Beating a Path to an Indoor Fruit Garden in Less Than 30 Days

Greenhouse Planning for Year-Round Gardening. Grow Fruit Trees and Bushes Indoors. Create a Lasting Garden That Can Make You a Profit.
Gregory Collins

About the Author

Hi, I'm Greg and I'm pleased to welcome you to read my book on gardening. The main purpose of me writing a garden-centric book in the first place is because, simply put, I love gardening. It's such a wonderful way to get in touch with nature that I feel most of us tend to forget or lose touch with. There is such an incredible variety of fruits, vegetables, flowers, and spices to grow. So, so many in fact, it's well into the thousands for some, such as apples that have over 7,000 varieties!

My intentions are simple, to share my knowledge on gardening as well as to motivate or encourage you to try new gardening techniques or, if you're new, to start your very own sustainable garden. Personally, I'm a big fan of growing fruits. It's how I was brought up. My mother was an avid gardener, so I learned a lot from her and also from friends and neighbors.

However, when it came to me building my own garden, I can't say I had the best of starts myself. It's one thing to watch others do it, but entirely different when you start up from scratch. I did make a few mistakes here and there, and over time I learned from those mistakes in order to build a robust and thriving garden of my own. The feeling of being able to enjoy the literal fruits of your labor, it is such an indescribable emotion. If I was to sum it up with one word, I would say it gives a strong sense of "satisfaction."

Hopefully, you take to heart what I've written to you so that you too can experience that same sense of pride and joy in your own home garden. And together, grow that garden from dirt to harvest.

Your Free Gift

Your gardening bonus on how you can budget, design, and organize your garden in less than 30 days is available now! Using the guide along with this book will help you to start your garden off strong. Download it for free at the website below:

www.gregorysgardens.com

Gardening Contents

Introduction

Imagine the joy of waking up on a frosty winter morning, padding over to your kitchen, and plucking a perfectly ripe, sun-kissed peach from a tree just steps away from your bedroom window.

It sounds like a scene from a quaint countryside retreat, doesn't it? Well, believe it or not, you can experience this slice of rustic bliss right in your own urban apartment or cozy suburban home.

Hi, I'm Gregory, a self-proclaimed plant skeptic turned indoor gardening enthusiast. Not long ago, I couldn't keep a cactus alive, let alone imagine growing my own fruits! However, driven by frustration over bland store-bought produce and a touch of curiosity, I took a leap into the world of indoor fruit gardening.

Little did I know that it would transform my kitchen into a thriving orchard and become an unexpected source of relaxation amidst life's daily hustle and bustle.

Let me share a story that captures the essence of why I became passionate about indoor fruit gardening. It all started with a failed attempt to grow tomatoes on my apartment balcony.

I had eagerly planted several tomato seedlings in a few pots, envisioning bountiful harvests of juicy tomatoes throughout the summer. However, despite my best efforts, my plants struggled. They grew spindly and yellow, and the few tomatoes they produced were tasteless and disappointing.

Frustrated, I almost gave up on gardening altogether.

One day, while browsing a local gardening store, I stumbled upon a small indoor lemon tree. Intrigued, I decided to give it a try. Armed with newfound determination and a bit of skepticism, I carefully selected a sunny spot in my living room and planted the lemon tree in a larger pot with nutrient-rich soil.

To my surprise and delight, the lemon tree thrived. Its glossy leaves shimmered in the sunlight, and before long, fragrant white blossoms appeared, promising the possibility of fruit. By this time, I had my fingers crossed and prayed to the garden gods to let my little lemon tree live.

Months passed, and I watched with awe as tiny green lemons began to appear and slowly matured into bright yellow fruits. The first time I plucked a lemon from my own tree and squeezed its tangy juice into a glass of water, I was hooked.

The flavor was incomparable to any lemon I had bought from a store—it was vibrant, zesty, and bursting with freshness. That experience sparked my journey into indoor fruit gardening, where I discovered the joy of growing my own food and the satisfaction of knowing exactly where it came from.

In today's fast-paced world, where the origins of our food are often obscured and the demand for healthier, more sustainable living continues to grow, indoor fruit gardening offers a refreshing solution.

You might be concerned about the chemicals in store-bought fruits, or maybe you just simply crave the satisfaction of nurturing something from seed to fruition. Whatever your reason, this book is your ultimate guide to going on a fruitful journey with confidence.

Within these pages, I'll walk you through everything you need to know to kickstart your indoor fruit garden adventure, whether you're a novice with a notorious black thumb or a seasoned gardener looking to bring the outdoors inside.

From setting up your indoor garden space to selecting the perfect fruit varieties that thrive in confined environments, consider this book your companion on the path to homegrown success.

Ever wondered how to coax a lemon tree to thrive in your living room or coax strawberries to bear fruit in a sunny corner? Fear not, we'll cover all that and more.

Also, you're probably wondering why you, of all people, should take on this indoor gardening adventure. Well, just imagine the satisfaction of plucking your own vine-ripened tomatoes in the dead of winter or savoring pesticide-free strawberries whenever you please.

Indoor fruit gardening isn't just about delicious rewards; it's about reclaiming control over what goes into your food and reconnecting with the natural world. With your own indoor garden, you can ensure your fruits are bursting with flavor and nutrients, unlike their mass-produced counterparts that lose their essence during long journeys from farm to store shelf.

You'll be surprised at how many people can do this. All it requires is a bit of curiosity about growing your own food in the most unexpected places—whether you live in a bustling city apartment with limited space or a suburban home with a sunlit nook to spare.

It doesn't matter either, whether you're seeking a therapeutic hobby to unwind after a hectic day or a sustainable way to supplement your grocery runs; indoor fruit gardening offers a rewarding escape.

Throughout these chapters, we'll delve into the essentials of indoor gardening, from selecting the right containers and soil mixes to mastering the art of pollination and managing pests.

Worried about pesky insects invading your beloved plants or uncertain about the best ways to store your harvest? Don't worry, we'll cover those topics and more.

Beyond the practical aspects, indoor fruit gardening nurtures more than just plants; it cultivates a sense of accomplishment and well-being. Research shows that tending to plants reduces stress, boosts mood, and fosters a sense of responsibility—qualities we all crave in our fast-paced lives.

After all, nothing brings a unique sense of pride and a deeper connection to nature than nurturing a tiny avocado seedling or coaxing a fig tree into bearing fruit.

So, join me on this journey to cultivate your own indoor fruit garden. Together, we'll sow the seeds of a healthier, more sustainable lifestyle and lose ourselves in the joy of eating homegrown goodness year-round.

Starting small with a few pots on your balcony, or dreaming big with a full-fledged indoor orchard? It doesn't matter. This book will be your go-to resource.

Remember, this is a relaxing yet committed project. Mistakes are perfectly fine—consider them as learning opportunities.

The main goal is to enjoy the journey and take pride in your efforts.

Now, let's transform your space into a thriving oasis of fresh, organic fruits—because why settle for bland store-bought fruits when you can harvest your own flavorful bounty?

Come along, and let's begin this journey together from dirt to harvest!

Chapter One

Where Do I Start in Building a Greenhouse?

WHETHER YOU'RE A SEASONED gardener or a newbie with a green thumb itching to sprout, this chapter is for you. We'll cover everything you need to know to get started with your indoor or greenhouse garden within 30 days. If it takes you a little longer, that is perfectly fine. Remember, the goal is to enjoy the process and take pride in your gardening journey.

Section 1: Planning and Designing Your Space

Growing plants indoors isn't just about bringing some in and hoping for the best. It involves careful planning and consideration, and understanding the ultimate benefits of having greenery indoors.

This step is usually what takes the longest along with obtaining materials. However, if done efficiently, this should take you around 14-18 days to plan, budget, and obtain all you need to start building.

Benefits of Building a Greenhouse

Building a greenhouse extends your growing season, protects plants from harsh weather, and allows you to grow a wider variety of fruits. It creates a controlled environment for gardening, making it easier to manage pests and diseases.

Additionally, greenhouses can be aesthetically pleasing, adding value and beauty to your property. The controlled environment also helps in experimenting with different gardening techniques, giving you a fulfilling and rewarding gardening experience.

Why Have a Garden?

Gardening offers numerous benefits beyond just growing your own food. It's a therapeutic activity that can reduce stress, improve mental health, and provide physical exercise.

Growing your own fruits ensures that you have access to fresh, organic produce, which is healthier and often tastier than store-bought options. Gardening also promotes sustainability by reducing your carbon footprint and fostering a closer connection to nature.

What to Consider When Starting

When starting a garden, think about such factors as available space, light conditions, soil quality, and water access. Decide what types of fruits you want to grow and research their specific requirements. Take into account your local climate and how it will affect your plants.

Budgeting is also crucial; determine how much you're willing to invest in your garden. Planning includes choosing the right location for your garden or greenhouse and considering the time you can dedicate to gardening.

Types of Greenhouses

There are various types of greenhouses to suit different needs and spaces. Each type has its own set of advantages, so choose one that best fits your space, budget, and gardening goals.

- Freestanding Greenhouses – These can be placed anywhere in your yard and offer flexibility in size and design.

- Lean-to Greenhouses – These attach to an existing building, saving space and often using the building's wall for added support.

- Mini Greenhouses – Ideal for small spaces or beginners, these are compact and perfect for starting seeds or growing a few plants.

- Cold Frames and Hotbeds – These are smaller structures that extend the growing season by protecting plants from cold weather.

- Passive Solar Greenhouses – Cost-effective and Eco-friendly greenhouses such as hoop houses, are ideal for moderate climates to maintain a stable temperature and minimize heating needs.

Basics on Setting Up a Greenhouse

Setting up a greenhouse involves choosing the right location, ensuring proper ventilation, and managing temperature and humidity. First, select a site with plenty of sunlight, preferably south-facing. It's best to use materials like polycarbonate panels or glass for durability and insulation.

Then, install vents or fans to ensure good airflow and prevent overheating. Finally, plan the layout to maximize space and make maintenance easier, incorporating shelves, benches, and paths.

Potential Costs

The cost of setting up a greenhouse varies depending on size, materials, and additional features. Basic DIY greenhouses can be built for a few hundred dollars, while larger, more sophisticated ones can cost several thousand.

Look at costs for materials, tools, heating, cooling, and irrigation systems. Budgeting ahead helps manage expenses and ensures you don't encounter unexpected costs.

Budget Gardening

Gardening can be affordable with a bit of creativity. Start small and expand as you gain experience. Use recycled materials, such as old containers for pots and homemade compost. Look for sales and second-hand tools to reduce costs.

Consider starting with inexpensive, easy-to-grow plants and gradually adding more as your budget allows. With resourcefulness, you can create a beautiful garden without spending a fortune.

Selecting Materials

Choose durable and appropriate materials for your greenhouse and gardening needs. For the structure, materials like aluminum or treated wood for the frame and polycarbonate or glass for the panels are recommended.

For soil, use high-quality potting mixes that provide good drainage and nutrients. Invest in basic gardening tools, such as a trowel, watering can, and pruning shears. Quality materials ensure longevity and the success of your gardening efforts.

When is the Right Time to Start?

The best time to start planning your garden is during the off-season, such as winter, when you can take time to research and gather materials. For planting, early spring is generally ideal for most fruits.

But with a greenhouse, you can start earlier or extend the growing season into fall and winter. Timing depends on the specific needs of the plants you choose and your local climate conditions.

Sloped Landscape Building

Building a greenhouse on a sloped landscape requires careful planning. Ensure the structure is level by building terraces or retaining walls. This prevents water runoff and soil erosion.

Sloped sites can offer advantages, such as improved drainage and better sunlight exposure. With proper planning, a sloped landscape can be an excellent location for a greenhouse, enhancing its functionality and aesthetics.

Building on a Budget

To build a greenhouse on a budget, think about using cost-effective materials like PVC pipes and polyethylene film. DIY kits and second-hand materials can also save money.

Focus on essential features like ventilation and insulation, and add upgrades gradually as your budget allows. Building incrementally allows you to spread costs over time and make improvements as needed.

Best Time to Plan

Winter is an excellent time to plan your garden. Use this period to design your layout, research plants, and gather materials. By the time spring arrives, you'll be ready to start planting. Planning ahead allows you to take advantage of seasonal sales and ensures you're prepared for the growing season.

Various Greenhouse Building Methods

There are numerous ways to build a greenhouse, from simple DIY projects to professional installations. Decide on the size and style that fit your needs, whether it's a small cold frame or a large walk-in structure.

Think about features like automatic vent openers, irrigation systems, and grow lights. Customize your greenhouse to suit your gardening style and preferences, ensuring it meets your needs and budget.

Permits May Be Required

Before building a greenhouse, check local regulations. Some areas require permits for structures over a certain size. Compliance with local codes ensures your greenhouse is safe and legally sound.

Consult with local authorities or a professional builder to understand the requirements in your area, avoiding potential legal issues and ensuring your project proceeds smoothly.

Section 2: Building and Setting Up Greenhouses

Now that everything's ready, you can begin building and setting up your greenhouse. Building a greenhouse is an exciting step in creating a productive garden space that extends your growing season. Depending on the size and materials used, can be assembled within a single weekend or 2-4 days.

Building a Greenhouse

You can choose from various greenhouse types, including freestanding, lean-to, and hoop houses, each suited to different needs and budgets. If you decide to add more, you can always build further to your greenhouse.

When planning your greenhouse, think about the size and location. Ensure it receives ample sunlight, ideally 6-8 hours of direct sunlight per day. The structure should be sturdy enough to withstand local weather conditions, from heavy snow to strong winds.

Including shelves is a great way to maximize space in a tiny area. You can fill your shelf space with smaller potted plants, just make sure you allow plenty of space above each shelf.

Building a Wooden Greenhouse

If you decide on a wooden greenhouse, you'll need to gather specific materials like treated lumber for durability, screws, nails, and clear polycarbonate panels for the walls and roof. A wooden greenhouse is aesthetically pleasing and can be customized to fit your garden's style.

Start by constructing a solid foundation, which could be a concrete slab or treated wood. Next, frame the structure, install the panels, and ensure proper ventilation and door access. The process might take a few days to weeks, depending on the complexity of the design.

Heating Selection

Choosing the right heating method for your greenhouse is crucial, especially if you plan to grow year-round. Options include electric heaters, propane heaters, and passive solar heating. Each has its pros and cons in terms of cost, installation, and maintenance.

For instance, electric heaters are easy to install but can be costly to run, while propane heaters are efficient but require ventilation to prevent gas buildup. Passive solar heating, using water barrels or thermal mass, can be cost-effective but might not provide consistent heat during cold spells.

Unheated Winter Growing

An unheated greenhouse can still be productive during winter if you grow cold-tolerant crops like spinach, kale, and carrots. These plants can thrive in cooler temperatures and benefit from the greenhouse's protection against frost.

Techniques, such as using row covers inside the greenhouse, can further insulate plants and extend the growing season. Be prepared to monitor temperature fluctuations and provide additional protection during extreme cold.

Recommended Building Tools

To build a greenhouse, you'll need essential tools, such as a tape measure, leveler, hammer, and screwdrivers for precise construction. Along with nails, screws, caulk, and wood glue to fasten everything  together. A saw and wrench set are also crucial for assembling the structure. Power tools like drills or band saws will help in making the building process a bit easier.

Additionally, having a shovel, post hole digger, and concrete mixer can help with preparing the foundation and securing the greenhouse.

Make certain you have personal protective equipment like goggles, thick gloves, steel toed boots, and if necessary, ear plugs.

Remember, investing in quality tools will ensure a smooth building process and a durable greenhouse. Properly storing these tools in a designated area can help keep them in good condition and readily accessible.

Lighting (Natural vs. Artificial)

Lighting is crucial for plant growth, especially during shorter winter days. While natural sunlight is ideal, artificial grow lights can supplement light during cloudy days or extend daylight hours. LED grow lights are energy-efficient and can be customized to provide the specific light spectrum plants need.

When setting up artificial lighting, ensure it mimics the natural day-night cycle to avoid stressing the plants. Properly placed lights can also help evenly distribute light to all plants in the greenhouse.

Watering

Efficient watering is vital for healthy plant growth in a greenhouse. Drip irrigation systems are highly effective, delivering water directly to the plant roots and reducing evaporation. Alternatively, you can use a soaker hose or traditional watering cans.

Monitor soil moisture regularly to prevent over or under-watering. Automated watering systems with timers can ensure consistent watering, especially during vacations or busy periods. Collecting and using rainwater is another sustainable option for your greenhouse.

Humidity Control

Maintaining the right humidity level in your greenhouse is essential to prevent plant diseases like mold and mildew. Ventilation is the primary method of controlling humidity. Installing vents, fans, and windows that can be opened helps regulate air circulation.

In more advanced setups, you can use dehumidifiers or humidity controllers. Regularly monitoring humidity levels with a hygrometer ensures your plants stay healthy. Adjusting watering schedules and using mulch can also help manage humidity.

Advanced Setup (Solar Panels)

Incorporating solar panels into your greenhouse setup can be an excellent way to make your gardening more sustainable.

Solar panels can power ventilation systems, automatic watering systems, and lighting.

This setup reduces reliance on external power sources and lowers your carbon footprint. While the initial investment can be high, the long-term savings and environmental benefits make it worthwhile. Consult with a solar energy specialist to design a system that meets your greenhouse's energy needs.

Section 3: Indoor Gardening Setups

There are many things to consider when setting up your indoor garden as part of your planning phase. Let's look at the most basic ones.

Essential Gardening Tools

To ensure your indoor gardening setup is effective, it's crucial to have the right tools. Basic gardening tools include a trowel, pruning shears, and a watering can. Additionally, specialized tools like soil thermometers, humidity meters, and grow lights are essential for indoor setups.

These tools help monitor and maintain the optimal growing environment for your plants. Investing in quality equipment can make a significant difference in the success of your indoor garden.

Shelves in Greenhouse

 Maximizing space is key in an indoor gardening setup, and installing shelves can help you make the most of the available area. Shelving units allow you to grow more plants vertically and organize them according to their light and water needs.

Sturdy, adjustable shelves are ideal as they can be reconfigured to accommodate different plant sizes and growth stages. Use materials that resist moisture and support the weight of pots and plants.

Tents

Grow tents are an excellent option for indoor gardening, providing a controlled environment that can optimize plant growth. These tents are typically lined with reflective material to enhance light distribution and come with built-in ventilation systems.

They are particularly useful for growing plants that require specific light and humidity conditions. Setting up a grow tent involves choosing the right size for your space, installing lights, and ensuring proper ventilation.

Pots and Containers

Choosing the right pots and containers is crucial for indoor gardening. Pots come in various sizes and materials, each with its benefits. Plastic pots are lightweight and affordable, while ceramic pots are more decorative and provide better insulation.

Ensure that all containers have drainage holes to prevent waterlogging, which can harm plant roots. For those with limited space, vertical planters and hanging baskets can be effective solutions.

What You Can Grow in Containers

Indoor gardening allows for a wide range of plants, including herbs, vegetables, and even small fruit trees. Herbs like basil, parsley, and mint thrive in pots and can be grown on windowsills or shelves.

Vegetables, such as tomatoes, peppers, and lettuce, can also be successfully grown in containers with the right care. For those interested in fruit, dwarf varieties of citrus trees or strawberries are excellent choices for indoor growing.

Selecting Pots

When selecting pots, consider the size and type of plant you plan to grow. Larger plants need bigger pots to accommodate their root systems, while smaller plants can thrive in smaller containers.

The material of the pot can also affect plant health. Terra cotta pots are breathable and prevent root rot, but they can dry out quickly. Self-watering pots are a great option for those who may forget regular watering.

Hanging Baskets

Hanging baskets are a creative way to add greenery to indoor spaces without taking up floor space. Plants like strawberries, cherry tomatoes, and various herbs grow well in hanging baskets. These baskets can be  hung near windows to maximize light exposure. Ensure the baskets are securely fastened and have good drainage to maintain plant health.

Raised Beds Basics and Setup

Raised beds can be used indoors to create a mini garden. These beds provide better control over soil quality and drainage, and they can be built to fit various spaces. Use untreated wood or metal frames to construct the beds, and fill them with a high-quality soil mix.

Raised beds are particularly useful for growing root vegetables like carrots and radishes, as they provide deep, loose soil for roots to develop.

Types of Raised Beds and Setup

Raised beds can be constructed from various materials, including wood, metal, and plastic. Each material has its pros and cons.

Wooden beds are easy to build and blend well with indoor decor but may need to be replaced after several years. Metal beds are durable and resistant to rot but can be more expensive. Plastic beds are lightweight and long-lasting but may not be as aesthetically pleasing.

Types of Soil Setups

Using the right soil mix is crucial for indoor gardening success. For most indoor plants, a lightweight, well-draining potting mix is ideal. You can create your mix by combining peat moss, perlite, and compost.

Adding vermiculite can help retain moisture without compacting the soil. Ensure the soil is free from pests and diseases by purchasing sterilized potting soil from reputable suppliers.

Benefits of Raised Beds

Raised beds offer numerous benefits, including improved soil quality, better drainage, and easier access for planting and harvesting. They can help reduce the presence of weeds and pests, making gardening more manageable.

Raised beds also warm up faster in the spring, allowing for an earlier start to the growing season. Indoors, they can be placed near windows or under grow lights to provide optimal growing conditions.

Cons of Raised Beds

While raised beds offer many advantages, there are also some drawbacks to consider. Building raised beds can be more expensive than traditional gardening methods, and they require regular maintenance to ensure the soil remains fertile. However, the benefits often outweigh the disadvantages, particularly for those with limited outdoor space or poor soil conditions.

Best Selections of Fruits for Containers

Certain fruits are particularly well-suited for container gardening. Dwarf fruit trees, such as lemons, limes, and figs, can thrive in pots with proper care.

Berries like strawberries, blueberries, and raspberries are also excellent choices for containers. These plants can produce abundant harvests in a small space, making them ideal for indoor gardening.

DIY Raised Beds

Building your raised beds can be a rewarding DIY project. Start by selecting a suitable location and measuring the area to determine the bed size. Use untreated wood or other safe materials to construct the frame, and line the bottom with landscape fabric to prevent weeds.

Fill the bed with a high-quality soil mix, and you're ready to plant. Raised beds can be customized to fit any space and can be painted or stained to match your indoor decor.

FAQs

Many common questions arise when setting up an indoor garden.

For instance, how often should you water indoor plants? It varies by plant type, but most indoor plants prefer to dry out slightly between waterings.

What type of light is best? Natural sunlight is ideal, but grow lights can supplement if necessary.

Can you grow plants from seeds indoors? Absolutely! Starting seeds indoors is a great way to get a jump on the growing season.

Do you need to have the greenhouse built without a floor? The answer is no, you can have flooring for your greenhouse, just make sure there is plenty of drainage to prevent standing water from building up.

Can you reuse the water from hanging plants? You can, but you should first collect then dilute the plant water with fresh water. Different soils have different properties and what is healthy for one plant could be harmful to another.

What can you do if you're not able to build a greenhouse yourself? There are contractors that you can always hire that can assemble it for you. Keep in mind, this will increase the overall costs.

Troubleshooting

Indoor gardening comes with its own set of challenges. Common issues include pests, such as aphids and spider mites, which you can control with insecticidal soap or neem oil.

Overwatering is another frequent problem that can result in root rot. To avoid this, ensure proper water drainage and monitor soil moisture levels to prevent this. If plants are not thriving, check for adequate light and adjust as needed.

Common Mistakes

Overcrowding plants can lead to poor air circulation and increased disease risk. Make sure each plant has enough space to grow.

Neglecting to adjust light and watering needs as seasons change can also impact plant health.

Overfertilizing is another issue that you can fix by following the product usage instructions. Remember to regularly assess and adjust your gardening practices to meet your plants' needs.

Chapter Two
Picking the Right Fruits

WHEN STARTING AN INDOOR fruit garden, the first crucial step is selecting the right type of fruits. Not all fruits are suitable for container gardening or greenhouse cultivation.

Section 1: Ideal and Not-So-Good Plants

Choosing the right plants can lead to a bountiful harvest, while the wrong choices might result in frustration and wasted resources. This section will guide you through which fruits are ideal for indoor gardening and which ones are best avoided. Selecting and obtaining your fruit plants should take up to 4-6 days. It may take longer if you order plants online.

Ideal Fruits for Containers and Greenhouses

 Growing fruits in containers or greenhouses offers flexibility and can lead to a rewarding harvest. Here are some top choices for indoor fruit gardening.

Strawberries

Excellent for containers and hanging baskets. They require minimal space and can produce fruit throughout the growing season.

Blueberries

With the right acidic soil, blueberries can thrive in containers and provide a generous yield.

Dwarf Citrus Trees

Dwarf varieties of citrus trees, such as lemons, limes, and oranges, can do well in pots and add a vibrant, fresh element to your indoor garden.

Tomatoes

Technically a fruit, tomatoes can be incredibly productive in containers with proper support and sunlight.

Figs

Fig trees can adapt well to container life and produce sweet fruits in a sunny indoor spot.

Peppers

Another fruit often mistaken for a vegetable, peppers can thrive in pots and provide colorful and spicy yields.

Raspberries

Dwarf varieties can be grown in large pots and provide a delicious summer treat.

Blackberries

Similar to raspberries, these can be grown in containers with proper support and care.

Grapes

Dwarf grapevines can be grown in pots and trained to grow vertically, saving space.

Cherries

Dwarf cherry trees can produce abundant fruit in a container setting.

Gooseberries

These can be grown in pots and provide tart, flavorful fruits.

Currants

Both red and black currants can thrive in containers and offer a unique addition to your fruit garden.

Kumquats

These small citrus fruits are well-suited for container growing.

Mulberries

Dwarf mulberry trees can be grown in pots and provide sweet, dark berries.

Pineapples

While a bit unconventional, pineapples can be grown in containers and offer a tropical touch to your indoor garden.

Fruits to Avoid

 While many fruits can adapt to container and greenhouse growing, some are not well-suited for these environments due to their size, root structure, or specific growing needs.

You may be able to grow some in this list if you have a large enough greenhouse or can find smaller growing varieties.

Apples

Standard apple trees require more space and deep root systems that containers cannot provide. However, some dwarf varieties might be manageable with careful planning.

Pears

Like apples, pear trees generally need more space than containers can offer.

Peaches

Standard peach trees have extensive root systems and require ample space to grow properly.

Nectarines

Similar to peaches, nectarines are best suited for open ground rather than containers.

Plums

Plum trees typically require more space and deep roots.

Watermelons

Watermelons need extensive space and support for their sprawling vines, making them less ideal for container gardening.

Cantaloupes

Like watermelons, cantaloupes have sprawling vines that require significant space.

Pumpkins

Pumpkins need a lot of space and deep soil to grow well.

Papayas

Papaya trees grow very tall and require more space than most indoor environments can provide.

Avocados

Avocado trees typically grow too large for containers and need specific conditions that are hard to replicate indoors.

Section 2: Companion Planting and Grouping

Companion planting is a valuable technique in gardening that involves grouping plants together to enhance growth, deter pests, and maximize space. By understanding which plants work well together, you can create a more efficient and productive indoor fruit garden.

This section will explore companion planting for the fifteen ideal fruits listed previously and identify combinations to avoid.

- **Strawberries** benefit from being planted alongside borage and spinach. Borage helps improve the flavor and yield of strawberries, while spinach makes efficient use of the ground space. However, strawberries should not be planted near cabbage or cauliflower, as these vegetables can stunt their growth.

- **Blueberries** thrive when planted with herbs like thyme and basil. These herbs can improve soil health and repel pests that might otherwise harm blueberries. Avoid planting blueberries near tomatoes, as both are susceptible to the same pests and diseases, which can easily spread.

- **Citrus trees**, such as lemons and limes, grow well with nasturtiums and marigolds. These companion plants attract beneficial insects and repel pests. However, keep citrus trees away from carrots and dill, as these can attract pests that harm citrus plants.

- **Tomatoes** pair well with basil and marigolds. Basil enhances the flavor of tomatoes and repels pests like whiteflies, while marigolds deter nematodes and other harmful insects. Avoid planting tomatoes near corn and potatoes, as these combinations can lead to pest infestations and disease transmission.

- **Figs** benefit from the presence of mint and nasturtiums. Mint can repel pests like ants and aphids, while nasturtiums act as a trap crop for aphids. Do not plant figs near legumes like beans and peas, as they can interfere with the nutrient uptake of fig trees.

- **Peppers** grow well with onions and carrots. Onions help repel pests that commonly affect peppers, and carrots make efficient use of the soil space. Peppers should not be planted near fennel, as it can inhibit their growth.

- **Raspberries** thrive alongside garlic and chives. These companion plants help deter pests, such as aphids and spider mites. However, avoid planting raspberries near potatoes, as this can increase the risk of disease.

- **Blackberries** pair well with mint and rue. Mint can

help repel pests, while rue acts as a deterrent for insects that might damage blackberries. Do not plant blackberries near eggplants, as they can compete for nutrients and space.

- **Grapes** grow best with clover and beans. Clover improves soil nitrogen levels, and beans can climb the grapevines, making efficient use of vertical space. Avoid planting grapes near radishes and cabbage, as these can attract pests harmful to grapes.

- **Cherries** benefit from being planted with garlic and marigolds. Garlic helps repel aphids and borers, and marigolds attract beneficial insects. Cherries should not be planted near tomatoes and peppers, as these combinations can lead to disease transmission.

- **Gooseberries** thrive with mint and thyme. Mint repels pests like aphids, and thyme can help improve soil health. Avoid planting gooseberries near blackcurrants, as they can attract the same pests.

- **Currants**, both red and black, grow well with chives and garlic. These companion plants help deter pests and improve soil conditions. Do not plant currants near fennel, as it can inhibit their growth.

- **Kumquats** pair well with dill and nasturtiums. Dill attracts beneficial insects, and nasturtiums act as a trap crop for aphids. Avoid planting kumquats near potatoes and tomatoes, as they can share common pests and diseases.

- **Mulberries** benefit from being planted with garlic and marigolds. Garlic helps deter pests, and marigolds attract beneficial insects. Mulberries should not be planted near black walnut trees, as the juglone toxin from black walnut roots can inhibit their growth.

- **Pineapples** grow well with beans and tarragon. Beans fix nitrogen in the soil, which pineapples can benefit from, and tarragon can repel pests. Avoid planting pineapples near corn, as they can compete for space and nutrients.

Section 3: Growing Fruit Bushes and Trees

Growing fruit bushes and trees indoors can be a rewarding endeavor, providing fresh produce and a touch of nature to your living space. This section offers detailed instructions on the basics of growing fruit bushes and trees, emphasizing specific care practices to ensure healthy and fruitful plants.

Basics of Growing Fruit Bushes and Trees

To begin, selecting the right variety of fruit bushes and trees is crucial. For indoor gardens, consider dwarf or semi-dwarf varieties, as they are more manageable and suitable for confined spaces. Ensure your chosen plants are compatible with your climate and indoor conditions.

Watering Plants

Each type of fruit plant has unique water requirements based on factors like species, container size, soil type, and environmental conditions. Here's a quick breakdown.

- **Citrus trees (e.g., lemons and limes):** These plants prefer consistently moist but not waterlogged soil. Overwatering can lead to root rot, while underwatering can cause leaf drop.

- **Berry bushes (e.g., strawberries, blueberries, raspberries, blackberries):** These need regular watering, especially during fruiting periods. Blueberries, in particular, prefer acidic, well-draining soil.

- **Tomatoes and peppers:** These plants require consistent moisture but should not sit in soggy soil. Uneven watering can lead to issues like blossom end rot.

- **Grapes and mulberries:** These plants are relatively

drought-tolerant once established but need regular watering during their initial growth and fruiting stages.

- **Pineapples and figs:** These prefer slightly drier conditions compared to other fruit plants but still need regular watering to keep the soil evenly moist.

Best Practices for Watering

Proper watering is a critical component in ensuring the health and productivity of your indoor fruit bushes and trees. Let's go over the basics.

Deep Watering

Water deeply to ensure the entire root system is hydrated. This encourages roots to grow deeper, making the plant more resilient to dry conditions.

For containers, water until you see water draining out of the bottom. This indicates that the soil is thoroughly saturated.

Frequency

Watering frequency depends on the plant type, container size, and environmental conditions. Generally, most indoor fruit plants need watering once the top inch of soil feels dry.

During hot or dry periods, you may need to water more frequently. Conversely, during cooler, more humid periods, watering can be reduced.

Consistency

Maintain a consistent watering schedule to prevent stress on the plants. Irregular watering can lead to issues like fruit splitting or dropping.

Morning Watering

Watering in the morning allows the plants to absorb moisture before the heat of the day. It also ensures that any excess water on the leaves can evaporate, reducing the risk of fungal diseases.

Watering Techniques

The right watering techniques can prevent issues like root rot, nutrient deficiency, and stress on the plants. Here are several methods for watering your plants.

Manual Watering

Use a watering can with a narrow spout to direct water at the base of the plant, avoiding wetting the leaves.

For larger containers, a hose with a gentle spray nozzle can be used.

Drip Irrigation

Drip irrigation systems deliver water directly to the soil at a slow, steady rate, which is ideal for maintaining consistent moisture levels.

Set up a drip irrigation system with emitters placed near the base of each plant. Adjust the flow rate based on the plant's water needs.

Self-Watering Containers

These containers have a reservoir at the bottom that allows plants to absorb water as needed through capillary action.

Check and refill the reservoir regularly to ensure a constant supply of water.

Rain Barrels

Collecting rainwater is an eco-friendly way to water your plants. Use a rain barrel to capture and store rainwater, and then transfer it to your plants as needed.

Ensure the rain barrel is covered to prevent mosquito breeding and debris accumulation.

Common Watering Mistakes to Avoid

New gardeners are more prone to these mistakes, but it doesn't mean experienced growers aren't averse to committing them from time to time.

Overwatering – one of the most common mistakes and can lead to root rot, especially in containers with poor drainage. Always check soil moisture before watering.

Underwatering – can cause plants to become stressed, leading to poor fruit production and increased susceptibility to pests and diseases. Ensure the soil is consistently moist but not soggy.

Poor Drainage – ensure all containers have drainage holes to allow excess water to escape. Use a well-draining potting mix to prevent water from pooling around the roots.

Neglecting Humidity – indoor environments can be dry, especially with heating or air conditioning. Some fruit plants benefit from higher humidity levels. Use a humidity tray or mist the plants occasionally to maintain adequate humidity.

Special Considerations for Different Plant Types

- **Citrus trees** prefer to slightly dry periods between watering. Ensure the potting mix is free-draining, and avoid letting the plant sit in water.

- **Berry bushes** require consistent moisture, especially during fruiting. Mulching can help retain soil moisture and reduce watering frequency.

- **Tomatoes and peppers** need to be watered deeply and regularly. Mulching can also help maintain even soil moisture.

- **Grapes** should be watered regularly during the initial growth phase and fruiting season. Reduce watering during dormant periods.

- **Pineapples** require less frequent watering. Allow the soil to dry out slightly between watering.

Planting and Caring for Fruit Trees

Successfully planting and caring for fruit trees indoors involves understanding the specific needs of each type of tree, preparing the right environment, and maintaining consistent care routines. Here's an in-depth guide to help you nurture healthy, productive indoor fruit trees:

Container Selection

When picking containers, size is important. Choose a container that is at least 18–24 inches (46–60 cm) in diameter and depth to provide ample space for root growth.

Your containers can be made of plastic, ceramic, or terracotta. Ensure they have adequate drainage holes to prevent waterlogging. Also, think about getting containers with wheels or a lightweight design for easy movement.

Soil and Planting Mix

Use a high-quality, well-draining potting mix. A mix specifically formulated for citrus or fruit trees is ideal. Ensure the soil mix includes components like perlite or sand to improve drainage and aeration. Add organic compost or well-rotted manure to enrich the soil with essential nutrients.

Light Requirements

Fruit trees require at least 6–8 hours of direct sunlight daily. Place them near south-facing windows or under grow lights if natural light is insufficient.

If you don't have enough natural sunlight, then you can use grow lights. Look for full-spectrum grow lights to supplement natural light. Position the lights about 6–12 inches (15–30 cm) above the plants and adjust as they grow.

Temperature and Humidity

Maintain a consistent temperature between 65–75°F (18–24°C). Avoid placing trees near drafts or heating vents.

Indoor environments can be dry. Use a humidity tray, mist the leaves regularly, or use a humidifier to maintain humidity levels around 40–50%.

Planting the Tree

The first thing you need to do is prepare the container. Place a layer of gravel or broken pottery at the bottom of the container to enhance drainage. Fill the container with potting mix up to about one-third full.

Next, remove the tree from its nursery pot, gently loosening the roots. Position the tree in the center of the container, ensuring the root ball is level with the container's rim. Fill in some spill around the plant's root ball with potting mix, and then pat the soil firmly yet gently as you go. Avoid burying the trunk.

Then, water the tree deeply and thoroughly after planting to settle the surrounding soil as this will eliminate any air pockets. Ensure excess water drains out of the bottom.

Caring for Indoor Fruit Trees

Water your tree deeply and consistently. Allow the top inch of soil to dry out between watering. Use a moisture meter to check soil moisture levels if unsure.

Use a balanced, slow-release fertilizer specifically formulated for fruit trees. Follow the product instructions for application rates and frequency. Supplement with organic options like compost tea or fish emulsion for added nutrients.

Regular pruning helps maintain the tree's shape, encourages healthy growth, and increases fruit production. Prune during the dormant season to remove dead or diseased branches and shape the tree.

When it comes to pollination, some fruit trees are self-pollinating, while others require cross-pollination. Hand pollination can be done using a small brush to transfer pollen between flowers.

Pruning Branches

Trimming old or sickly branches will help keep your fruit plants alive. This is another way of helping to shape your fruit tree in smaller spaces. Pruning will help encourage growth through the remaining branches. Make certain your

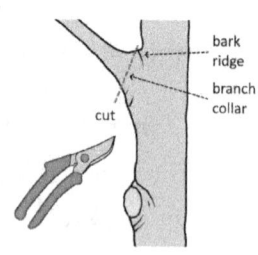

sheers are kept sharp and each time you finish use to sanitize them.

Seasonal Care

During the growing season, ensure the tree receives enough water and nutrients to support fruit development.

In winter, reduce watering and allow the tree to rest. Move it to a cooler location if necessary to mimic natural dormancy conditions.

Additional Tips

Rotate the container regularly to ensure even light exposure and balanced growth.

Use stakes or trellises to support young trees and prevent them from toppling over as they grow.

Harvest fruits when they are fully ripe. Each fruit type has specific indicators of ripeness, such as color change, firmness, or fragrance.

Repot the tree every 2–3 years to refresh the soil and provide more space for root growth. Choose a container that's a bit larger each time.

Updated Hardiness Zones

The USDA updated its Hardiness Zone Map in 2023 to reflect warming trends, shifting much of the US up by half a zone. These zones, divided into A and B subzones, help gardeners choose plants based on their cold tolerance. Refer to the back of this book for the layout of the USDA 2023 map.

Southern regions may need to consider heat and humidity separately, using the American Horticultural Society's heat zone map for more precise planting decisions.Using both maps ensures plants can thrive in local climates, enhancing gardening success.

Plant tags typically display a range of USDA Zones (e.g., Zones 6-9), indicating the plant's potential tolerance to different conditions within those zones. If a plant lacks a USDA Hardiness Zone number, it may not be suitable for your area and is likely intended as an annual elsewhere.

Chapter Three

Soil, Fertilizer, and Composting

WHEN I FIRST STARTED my indoor greenhouse, I was eager to see my plants flourish. I bought the most expensive potting soil and thought I had everything figured out. But soon, my enthusiasm turned to frustration. My tomato plants were stunted, and the leaves of my lemon tree turned yellow and fell off. I was confused and disheartened.

Determined to find out what went wrong, I dived into researching soil health and care. I discovered that I had overlooked the importance of soil pH and had chosen a soil mix unsuitable for my specific plants.

I learned how different plants require different soil types and how crucial it is to test and adjust soil pH. I also found out the importance of proper tilling and the benefits of composting for enriching soil.

With this newfound knowledge, I revamped my approach. I selected the right soil types, regularly tested and adjusted pH levels, and began composting. Gradually, my plants started to thrive. Now, I want to share these insights with you, so you can avoid the same mistakes and enjoy a bountiful indoor garden.

Section 1: Understanding Soil Needs

Unlike outdoor gardens, greenhouse environments require careful attention to soil composition, structure, and nutrients to optimize plant health and productivity. Here, we go into the basics of greenhouse soil management, covering preparation, types of soil, tilling practices, pH level testing, and considerations for potting soil in containers.

Basics and Preparation

Basics and preparation are foundational steps in creating a thriving indoor greenhouse environment. Starting with the right soil is important; it should be well-draining yet moisture-retentive, providing a stable medium for root growth.

Go for a high-quality potting mix designed for container gardening, ensuring it's sterile to prevent diseases and pests. If you're repurposing soil, amend it with organic matter like compost to improve its structure and fertility.

Understanding your plant's specific soil needs is essential. Some plants prefer slightly acidic soil, while others thrive in alkaline conditions. Conduct a soil pH test using a simple kit from your local garden center.

It's best to aim for a pH range that suits your chosen plants—typically around 6 to 7 for most fruits and vegetables. Adjust the pH accordingly with additives like sulfur for lowering pH or lime for increasing it.

Prepare your greenhouse bed or containers by loosening the soil to a depth of 6–8 inches. This step aids root penetration and allows for better water absorption. Think about adding a layer of gravel or broken pottery at the bottom of containers to improve drainage. Before planting, ensure the soil is well-aerated and free of weeds and debris.

Types of Soil

Choosing the right type of soil is important for greenhouse gardening success. Various soil types can be used depending on the plants and containers you are using.

For instance, potting soils are specifically formulated for container gardening, offering good drainage and aeration necessary for plant roots. A good potting mix typically consists of peat moss, perlite or vermiculite, and compost.

Peat moss retains moisture, perlite or vermiculite aids in drainage, and compost provides nutrients. Choose mixes labeled for specific plant types, such as citrus or succulents, to meet their unique needs.

Conversely, garden soils are suited for in-ground planting, providing more structure and nutrient retention. If using garden soil in containers, amend it with organic matter like compost to improve its texture and fertility. This helps mimic the nutrient-rich environment of natural soil while enhancing water retention and drainage.

For raised beds in your greenhouse, opt for a balanced soil mix that combines garden soil, compost, and a light-textured material like sand or perlite. This blend promotes root development and nutrient uptake, supporting healthier plant growth.

Tilling Soil

The practice of tilling soil in a greenhouse setting requires careful consideration. Unlike traditional outdoor gardens, greenhouse soils may not require deep tilling, especially if using raised beds or containers.

Tilling aids in soil aeration and loosening compacted soil, promoting better root penetration and water absorption. However, excessive tilling can disrupt soil structure and beneficial microorganisms.

pH Level Testing and Management

Before planting, test the soil pH using a kit to ensure it falls within the optimal range for your plants. Most fruits and vegetables prefer a slightly acidic to neutral pH (around 6 to 7), which can be adjusted using additives like lime or sulfur.

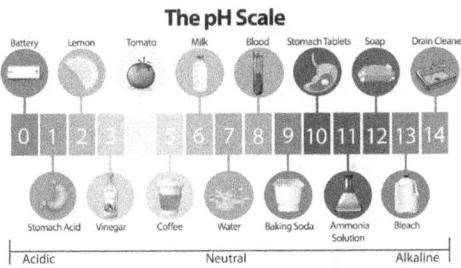

One should aim for a pH range suitable for the plants you are growing; for example, acidic soil for blueberries and alkaline soil for asparagus.

Section 2: Fertilizing and Mulching Your Indoor Garden

Thinking about mulching for your indoor garden? Mulching is a simple yet effective way to keep your indoor plants thriving year-round. Let's get to know more about mulching.

Choosing the Right Fertilizer

Selecting the appropriate fertilizer is important for maximizing plant health and productivity in your indoor greenhouse.

Here's a breakdown of different types of fertilizers and considerations.

Organic vs. Synthetic Fertilizers

Choosing between organic and synthetic fertilizers is a pivotal decision in greenhouse gardening, impacting both plant health and environmental sustainability. Organic fertilizers derive from natural sources like compost, manure, or plant residues.

They enhance soil structure, promote microbial activity, and release nutrients gradually, fostering long-term soil health. Organic options are preferred for their sustainability and minimal environmental impact.

Synthetic fertilizers, on the other hand, are chemically formulated to deliver specific nutrient ratios to plants quickly. They're often water-soluble, allowing for rapid nutrient uptake.

While effective for immediate plant growth, they can lead to nutrient imbalances, soil acidification, and reduced microbial activity over time. Synthetic fertilizers require careful application to avoid harming plants or contaminating groundwater.

When deciding between the two, consider your gardening goals and environmental concerns. Organic fertilizers support soil biodiversity and sustainability but may require more frequent applications.

Synthetic fertilizers offer quick results but necessitate precise usage to prevent negative environmental impacts. Ultimately, your choice should align with your greenhouse's specific needs, plant preferences, and commitment to sustainable gardening practices.

Slow-Release vs. Liquid Fertilizers

Choosing between slow-release and liquid fertilizers is important for maintaining optimal plant nutrition in your indoor greenhouse. Slow-release fertilizers provide nutrients gradually over an extended period, typically through coated pellets or granules.

They are convenient for busy gardeners as they require less frequent application, often lasting for several months. This type of fertilizer is ideal for plants that have steady nutrient requirements and prefer consistent feeding schedules.

On the other hand, liquid fertilizers offer immediate nutrient availability as they are quickly absorbed through plant roots and foliage. They are versatile and can be applied directly to the soil or as a foliar spray for rapid uptake. Liquid fertilizers are beneficial for plants that require frequent feeding or during periods of rapid growth, such as flowering or fruiting stages.

When deciding between the two, think about your plants' specific needs and growth stages. Slow-release fertilizers provide a steady supply of nutrients without the risk of over-fertilization, making them suitable for low-maintenance gardening.

Conversely, liquid fertilizers offer flexibility and immediate nutrient boost, which can be advantageous for quick corrections or targeted nutrient applications.

To use slow-release fertilizers effectively, apply them according to package instructions, usually at the beginning of the growing season or as directed. For liquid fertilizers, dilute them to the recommended concentration and apply evenly to avoid burning plant roots.

Regularly monitor plant health and adjust fertilization based on growth response and seasonal changes to maintain a balanced nutrient supply for thriving greenhouse plants.

DIY Fertilizers

Creating your own fertilizers can be a rewarding and cost-effective way to nourish your indoor greenhouse plants. Start by understanding the nutrient needs of your specific crops. Different plants require varying levels of nitrogen, phosphorus, and potassium, known as N-P-K, which are necessary for healthy growth.

Compost Tea

One straightforward method is to make a compost tea. To create compost tea, fill a bucket with water and add a mixture of kitchen scraps (like fruit and vegetable peels), yard waste (such as grass clippings and leaves), and other organic materials. Let the mixture steep for 3–5 days, stirring occasionally.

After steeping, strain the liquid through cheesecloth or a fine sieve. Dilute the tea with water until it resembles weak tea and use it to water your plants. This compost tea provides a balanced array of nutrients and beneficial microorganisms for healthy plant growth.

Egg Shells

Another option is to utilize kitchen scraps directly. Eggshells provide calcium, which is crucial for preventing blossom end rot in tomatoes and peppers. Save and dry  eggshells from your kitchen. Once dried, crush them into small pieces or grind them into a powder using a blender or mortar and pestle.

Sprinkle the crushed eggshells directly into the soil around calcium-loving plants like tomatoes and peppers. Alternatively, steep the crushed eggshells in water for a few days to create a calcium-rich solution. This DIY fertilizer helps prevent blossom end rot and promotes strong cell walls in plants.

Banana Peel Potassium Powder

Dry banana peels by cutting them into small pieces and leaving them in a sunny spot until fully dried. Once dried, grind the banana peels into a fine powder using a blender or food processor.

This powder can be sprinkled directly onto the soil or steeped in water to create a potassium-rich liquid fertilizer. Potassium is essential for fruit development and overall plant health, making this fertilizer beneficial for flowering and fruiting plants.

Coffee Grounds

For nitrogen-rich fertilizer, consider using coffee grounds. After brewing your coffee, spread the grounds around the base of your plants. They will gradually release nitrogen as they decompose, promoting healthy foliage growth.

Mulching Basics

Have you considered mulching for your indoor garden? Mulching is a simple yet effective way to keep your indoor plants thriving year-round. Plus, it's quite simple to do.

Benefits of Mulching

Mulching provides numerous benefits that contribute to the overall health and productivity of your indoor garden. First, mulch helps conserve soil moisture by reducing evaporation, which is crucial in a greenhouse environment where water can quickly evaporate due to higher temperatures. This moisture retention reduces the frequency of watering, thereby conserving water and ensuring plants receive consistent hydration.

Moreover, mulch acts as a natural insulator, regulating soil temperature fluctuations. In a greenhouse, this insulation is especially valuable as it helps keep the soil warmer during cooler periods and cooler during hot spells, providing a more stable environment for plant roots.

Weeds can be a persistent issue even indoors, but mulching suppresses any weed growth by blocking sunlight and preventing any unwanted weed seeds from growing. This reduces the need for manual weeding and keeps your indoor garden beds tidy.

Organic mulches, such as shredded leaves or bark chips, break down over time, enriching the soil with valuable nutrients and improving its structure. This natural decomposition process enhances soil fertility and promotes healthy microbial activity beneficial to plant growth.

Types of Mulch

Types of mulch play a vital role in maintaining soil health and enhancing plant growth in an indoor greenhouse setting. Mulch serves multiple purposes, including conserving soil moisture, suppressing weeds, moderating soil temperature, and improving soil fertility as it breaks down. Here are some common types of mulch and their benefits.

- **Organic Mulches** – Materials like shredded bark, wood chips, and compost are popular organic mulches. They gradually decompose, enriching the soil with nutrients and improving its structure. Organic mulches also help retain moisture and regulate soil temperature, creating a favorable environment for plant roots.

- **Inorganic Mulches** – Examples include gravel, stones, and landscape fabric. Inorganic mulches do not break down, offering long-lasting weed suppression and moisture retention benefits. They are particularly useful in areas where aesthetics and durability are priorities.

Best Mulches for Different Plants

For fruit-bearing plants like tomatoes and peppers, opt for organic mulches, such as straw or shredded leaves. These materials not only regulate soil temperature but also enrich the soil as they decompose, providing essential nutrients.

Herbs and leafy greens benefit from fine-textured mulches, such as grass clippings or compost. These mulches help maintain consistent soil moisture levels while keeping weeds at bay.

Perennial flowers and ornamental plants thrive with decorative mulches like wood chips or bark. These materials not only enhance the aesthetic appeal of your greenhouse but also promote soil health by gradually decomposing and adding organic matter.

Avoid using mulches like plastic or rocks indoors, as they can interfere with soil moisture levels and root health in containers.

Applying Mulch

Start by selecting the right type of mulch for your plants and greenhouse setup—organic options like compost, shredded leaves, or straw are excellent choices for indoor gardening.

To apply mulch effectively, spread a layer around 2–3 inches thick evenly over the soil surface, leaving a gap around plant stems to prevent moisture-related diseases. Mulch should not touch plant stems directly to avoid rot or pest issues.

Replenish mulch periodically as it decomposes, typically every few months, to maintain its benefits.

When choosing mulch, think about the aesthetic appeal alongside functionality. Light-colored mulches can reflect light and heat, helping to keep soil cool in warmer months, while darker mulches absorb heat, beneficial during cooler periods. Regularly monitor mulch depth and condition to ensure it continues to provide optimal benefits for your indoor garden's soil health and plant growth.

Section 3: Composting Indoors

Composting is an invaluable practice for maintaining a healthy and productive indoor greenhouse. At its core, composting recycles organic waste, turning it into nutrient-rich soil amendment that enhances plant growth.

Benefits of Composting

One of the primary benefits of composting is the enrichment of soil. Compost adds essential nutrients like nitrogen, phosphorus, and potassium, which are needed for plant health.

This nutrient boost leads to more vigorous growth, increased yields, and better resistance to pests and diseases. Moreover, compost improves soil structure, enhancing its ability to retain moisture and drain excess water, creating an ideal environment for roots to thrive.

Composting also supports beneficial microorganisms that help break down organic matter and suppress harmful pathogens. These microorganisms promote a healthy soil ecosystem, which is vital for plant health. Additionally, compost acts as a natural mulch, helping to regulate soil temperature, retain moisture, and prevent erosion.

Another significant benefit is the reduction of household waste. Kitchen scraps, garden trimmings, and other organic materials can be diverted from landfills, reducing your environmental footprint. This practice not only helps the planet but also turns waste into a valuable resource for your greenhouse.

Composting Methods

When it comes to composting, there are two primary methods: traditional compost piles and indoor compost bins. Each method has its own advantages and considerations, making them suitable for different gardening setups and personal preferences.

Traditional Compost Piles

Traditional compost piles are an excellent option for those with ample outdoor space. This method involves creating a heap of organic waste materials directly on the ground or within a composting frame. The key to a successful compost pile is to maintain a balance between green materials (rich in nitrogen) and brown materials (rich in carbon).

Traditional compost piles can handle large volumes of organic waste and produce substantial amounts of compost. However, they require regular maintenance and may take several months to fully decompose.

Indoor Compost Bins

For those with limited outdoor space or who prefer a more controlled environment, indoor compost bins are an ideal solution. These bins are designed to fit within your home or greenhouse, making composting convenient and accessible year-round.

Indoor compost bins are compact, odor-free (when managed properly), and produce compost more quickly than traditional piles. They are perfect for urban gardeners or those who want to compost during winter months.

Setting Up an Indoor Composting System

Composting indoors can be a practical solution for gardeners with limited outdoor space. It allows you to recycle kitchen scraps and other organic waste into nutrient-rich compost, benefiting your plants and reducing landfill waste.

Choosing the Right Compost Bin

Selecting the appropriate compost bin is crucial for successful indoor composting. There are several types of compost bins to consider. When choosing a bin, think about the amount of waste you generate, the space you have available, and your willingness to maintain the system.

- **Worm Bins**, or Vermicomposting, are a highly efficient method of composting that uses specific types of worms to break down organic waste into rich, nutrient-dense compost known as worm castings. This method is particularly suitable for indoor composting due to its compact size and relatively odor-free process.

- **Bokashi Bins** use a fermentation process to break down organic waste, including items not typically composted like meat and dairy. This method produces a nutrient-rich liquid and pre-compost material that can be buried or added to traditional compost piles.

- **Aerobic Compost Bins** facilitate the decomposition of organic matter through the action of aerobic (oxygen-loving) bacteria. These bins are designed to promote air circulation, which accelerates the composting process and reduces odors.

Preparing the Compost Bin

Once you've selected a bin, place the bin in a convenient, accessible location with adequate ventilation and sealed off to prevent critters from getting into them.

Start with a layer of soil or finished compost at the bottom of the bin. This introduces beneficial microorganisms needed for decomposition.

Ensure your bin has proper ventilation holes and drainage to prevent odors and excess moisture buildup.

Adding Materials

To maintain a healthy compost bin, balance green (nitrogen-rich) and brown (carbon-rich) materials.

Green materials include fruit and vegetable scraps, coffee grounds, and green plant clippings. On the other hand, brown materials consist of dry leaves, shredded newspaper, cardboard, and wood chips.

When adding your materials, alternate layers of green and brown materials. Start with a layer of browns to create a base that absorbs excess moisture.

Chop or shred larger pieces of waste to speed up decomposition. Compost should be as moist as a wrung-out sponge. Add water during dry periods and brown materials during wet periods to maintain the right moisture balance.

Exclude meat, dairy, oily foods, diseased plants, and weeds that have gone to seed. These can create odors, attract pests, or introduce pathogens to your compost.

Maintain a ratio of about 3 parts brown materials to 1 part green materials. This balance promotes efficient decomposition and reduces odors.

Maintaining Your Indoor Compost Bin

Regular maintenance is key to a successful indoor composting system. To do this, regularly mix the compost to ensure oxygen circulates throughout the bin, which helps decompose materials faster and prevents odors.

Check the moisture level by squeezing a handful of compost. It should feel like a damp sponge. If too dry, add water or moist greens. If too wet, add dry browns.

Monitoring the temperature of your compost pile can help you gauge its progress. A temperature between 130°F and 160°F indicates active decomposition.

Depending on the bin type, compost can take several weeks to several months to mature. Once ready, the compost will be dark, crumbly, and earthy-smelling. Use a screen or sieve to separate finished compost from larger, undecomposed materials.

Tips for Specific Bins

For worm bins, feed the worms weekly and ensure they have a balance of greens and browns. Harvest worm castings (compost) every few months.

For Bokashi bins, add kitchen scraps and Bokashi bran, pressing down to remove air pockets. Drain the liquid regularly and use it as fertilizer. After fermentation, bury the contents in soil for further decomposition.

For aerobic bins, turn the compost weekly and monitor moisture levels to keep the process active and efficient.

Chapter Four
Planting Your Greenhouse Garden

REMEMBER THE STORY ABOUT my first attempt at indoor gardening and how it all started with a single tomato plant? I was full of enthusiasm, armed with a little pot and some seeds, envisioning a bounty of ripe tomatoes. But despite my best efforts, that poor plant never thrived.

Not one to give up easily, I decided to try again, this time with a lemon plant. I researched, adjusted my approach, and learned from my mistakes. Slowly but surely, my lemon plant began to grow. It wasn't long before I was rewarded with vibrant, healthy leaves and eventually, fragrant lemons.

This small success sparked my passion for indoor gardening, proving that with patience, persistence, and the right knowledge, anyone can turn their indoor space into a thriving garden. Now, I'm excited to share everything I've learned with you in this chapter, starting with the basics of planting and moving on to more advanced techniques. Let's get started.

Section 1: Basics of Planting

By understanding the basics of planting, you'll set a strong foundation for your indoor garden. Whether you're starting with seeds, saplings, bushes, or trees, these guidelines will help you nurture healthy, productive plants.

Seeds or Saplings

Starting your indoor garden can be both exciting and daunting, especially when it comes to deciding between seeds or saplings. Each option has its own benefits and challenges, and your choice will depend on your gardening goals and level of patience.

Seeds

Seeds offer a cost-effective way to start your garden and provide the satisfaction of nurturing a plant from its earliest stages. However, seeds require more time and care. You'll need to start them in seed trays or small pots, providing consistent moisture and warmth.

Seedlings are delicate and need protection from drafts and temperature fluctuations. Once they develop a couple of true leaves, they can be transplanted into larger pots or directly into your greenhouse soil.

Saplings

Saplings, or young plants, are an excellent choice if you want a head start. They are more robust and have already overcome the vulnerable seedling stage.

Transplanting saplings involves carefully moving them from their initial pots to your garden or larger containers. Ensure you handle the roots gently and water them well after transplanting to help them settle into their new environment.

Picking Seeds/Seedlings

Choosing the right seeds or seedlings is crucial for a successful indoor garden. Not all plants are suitable for greenhouse conditions, so it's important to pick varieties that thrive indoors.

When picking seeds, look for high-quality, organic options from reputable suppliers. Consider the plant's growth requirements, including light, temperature, and space. Heirloom seeds are a great choice for those who value plant heritage and flavor.

For seedlings, inspect them closely before purchasing. Healthy seedlings should have vibrant, green leaves without any yellowing or spots. Check the roots, which should be white and well-developed, not circling around the pot. Choose seedlings that are compact and sturdy rather than tall and leggy.

Transplanting

Transplanting is a delicate process that, when done correctly, can set the stage for robust plant growth. The key is to minimize transplant shock by handling the plants gently and ensuring they are well-hydrated.

To transplant, start by preparing the new site. Whether it's a larger pot or a spot in your greenhouse garden, make sure the soil is well-draining and enriched with compost. Dig a hole that is slightly larger than the plant's current container.

Carefully remove the plant from its pot by gently squeezing the sides and tipping it out, supporting the root ball with your hand. Place the plant in the hole, ensuring it's at the same depth it was in its original container. Fill in around the plant with soil, pressing down lightly to eliminate air pockets. Water thoroughly to help the plant settle.

About Bushes and Shrubs

Bushes and shrubs can be a fantastic addition to your indoor garden, providing structure and a continuous harvest of fruits. These plants typically require more space and careful planning regarding their placement.

When planting bushes, such as berry bushes, choose a location with plenty of light and good air circulation. These plants often need support structures, like trellises or stakes, to keep them upright and ensure proper fruit development. Regular pruning is essential to maintain their shape and encourage new growth.

For shrubs, such as citrus or other fruit-bearing varieties, ensure you provide large enough containers to accommodate their root systems.

Shrubs generally prefer slightly acidic soil and consistent watering. Adding mulch around the base can help retain moisture and regulate soil temperature.

Growing Fruit Trees

Growing fruit trees in a greenhouse is a rewarding endeavor that requires some specific care to ensure success. Dwarf varieties are particularly well-suited to indoor gardening due to their manageable size.

For potted fruit trees, use large containers with good drainage. The soil should be rich in organic matter and well-aerated. Position your fruit trees in a sunny spot, as most require at least six hours of direct sunlight daily.

Regular pruning helps maintain the tree's shape and encourages fruit production. Be mindful of pests and diseases, which can be more prevalent in the controlled environment of a greenhouse. Use organic pest control methods to keep your trees healthy.

Section 2: Advanced Planting Care and Tonics

Mastering advanced planting care techniques in your greenhouse elevates your gardening skills and enhances the productivity of your indoor garden. By incorporating these practices, you'll cultivate healthy, thriving plants that yield abundant fruit year-round.

Tonics for Plant Growth

Boosting plant growth with tonics or fertilizers can significantly enhance your indoor gardening success. These tonics provide essential nutrients that may be lacking in your greenhouse soil, promoting vigorous growth and robust plants.

All-season tonics are versatile options that provide a balanced blend of nutrients throughout the year. They're easy to apply and can be diluted according to package instructions. Look for organic formulations to minimize chemical exposure and support a healthy ecosystem in your greenhouse.

Apply tonics according to the specific needs of your plants. Some may benefit from monthly applications during the growing season, while others may require less frequent feeding. Always follow dosage recommendations to avoid over-fertilization, which can harm plants.

Nutrient Boost Tonic

- 1 cup of compost tea or liquid fertilizer

- 1 tablespoon of seaweed extract

- 1 teaspoon of Epsom salt.

Stir the mixture thoroughly in a gallon-sized container filled with water. Allow it to steep for 24 hours before straining out any solids. Dilute the tonic by mixing 1 part tonic with 10 parts water. Apply this tonic to the base of plants every 2–4 weeks during the growing season. Water plants deeply after application to help nutrients penetrate the soil and reach the roots effectively.

Vitamin-Infused Growth Tonic

- 1 tablespoon of fish emulsion or hydrolyzed fish fertilizer

- 1 teaspoon of liquid kelp extract

- 1 teaspoon of apple cider vinegar

Mix into a gallon jug filled with water. Shake well to blend the ingredients thoroughly. Let the mixture sit for 12–24 hours to allow the components to meld.

Before use, strain the tonic to remove any solids. Dilute the tonic with water at a ratio of 1 part tonic to 4 parts water. Apply the diluted tonic to the soil around plants once every 2 weeks during the growing season. Ensure even distribution and avoid over-fertilizing to prevent burning the plant roots.

Herbal Pest Repellent Tonic

- 1 cup of chopped garlic cloves

- 1 cup of chopped hot peppers (such as jalapenos)

- 1 tablespoon of neem oil

Add these ingredients to a gallon jug and fill it with warm water. Let the mixture steep for 24–48 hours to infuse the water with the natural oils and repellent properties of the herbs. Strain the liquid to remove solids before transferring it to a spray bottle. Spray the tonic directly onto plants affected by pests, focusing on the undersides of leaves and areas where pests are present.

Use caution when applying to sensitive plants and test a small area first to ensure there is no adverse reaction. Apply this herbal tonic every 1–2 weeks or as needed to control pests and protect your plants.

Tying Down Plants

Supporting plant growth with tying techniques helps prevent sprawling and encourages upward growth, optimizing space and light utilization in your greenhouse.

Tying up tomato plants, for example, involves gently securing the main stem to a stake or trellis as the plant grows. This prevents the stems from breaking under the weight of developing fruit and improves air circulation around the plant.

For vine plants, such as cucumbers or beans, consider using a sling to support their weight as they grow and produce fruit. This reduces the risk of branches snapping and ensures even ripening of fruits.

Experiment with different tying methods to find what works best for your plants and greenhouse setup. Soft materials like twine or plant ties are gentle on plant stems and allow for growth without constriction.

Anchoring Trees

Stabilizing trees in your greenhouse is crucial, especially for taller varieties or those prone to toppling over in windy conditions. Proper anchoring ensures the safety and longevity of your fruit trees.

Anchoring dwarf fruit trees involves securing them to a stake or support structure buried firmly in the soil. Use soft ties to attach the tree trunk to the anchor, allowing for some movement but preventing excessive swaying.

Monitor tree anchoring regularly, especially after severe weather, to ensure the ties remain secure and the tree continues to grow upright. Adjust ties as needed to accommodate trunk growth without causing damage.

Bending Branches

Bending branches is a technique used to shape fruit trees and promote better fruit production. This method encourages lateral growth and helps create a balanced canopy for optimal sunlight exposure.

Bend branches carefully during the dormant season when the tree is not actively growing. Use gentle pressure to guide branches into desired positions, securing them with ties or weights if necessary. Avoid bending branches that are brittle or likely to break.

Regularly inspect bent branches throughout the growing season to ensure they're growing in the desired direction. Prune any unwanted growth to maintain the tree's shape and encourage new fruit-bearing wood.

Grafting Branches

Grafting allows you to combine desirable traits from different fruit tree varieties onto a single tree, maximizing space and fruit diversity in your greenhouse.

Graft fruit tree branches during the dormant season using a sharp grafting knife to make clean cuts. Match the diameter of the scion (the cutting with desired traits) to the rootstock (the existing tree or seedling). Secure the graft with grafting tape or wax to promote healing and integration.

Choose compatible fruit varieties for grafting, considering factors like growth habits and disease resistance. Grafted trees may take several seasons to establish and produce fruit, but the results can be well worth the effort.

Growing Together

Companion planting is a strategic approach to maximize space and enhance plant health in your greenhouse. Certain plants have symbiotic relationships that benefit each other by repelling pests, attracting beneficial insects, or improving soil fertility.

Pair fruit trees with compatible herbs or flowers that deter common pests or provide natural pollination support. For example, planting marigolds near tomato plants can deter nematodes and attract pollinators.

Research companion planting guides specific to fruit trees and greenhouse gardening to find ideal plant combinations for your indoor garden. Experiment with different pairings to discover which combinations work best for your climate and growing conditions.

Pruning Trees

Pruning is a fundamental aspect of fruit tree care that promotes healthy growth, improves air circulation, and enhances fruit production in your greenhouse.

Prune fruit trees during the dormant season to remove dead or diseased branches, as well as those that cross or rub against each other. Use sharp pruning shears to make clean cuts just above a bud or branch collar.

Follow pruning guidelines specific to each fruit tree variety, as some may require different pruning techniques to shape and encourage fruiting wood. Regular pruning sessions help maintain tree structure and prevent overcrowding in your greenhouse.

Scheduling

Creating a seasonal planting calendar ensures year-round productivity and optimal growth conditions for your greenhouse plants.

Develop a greenhouse planting calendar that includes planting, watering, fertilizing, and harvesting schedules based on local climate conditions and plant growth requirements. Consider factors like temperature fluctuations, daylight hours, and humidity levels when planning your planting schedule.

Refer to gardening resources and local agricultural extension services for specific recommendations on greenhouse gardening schedules. Keep a gardening journal to track planting successes and challenges, adjusting your calendar as needed to optimize plant health and productivity.

You can also refer to your free gift that you can download from www.gregorysgardens.com for year-round garden planning.

Section 3: List and Care of Popular and Exotic Fruits

From familiar favorites like strawberries and blueberries to exotic delights like figs and soursop, this section is your passport to cultivating these treasures under controlled conditions.

Discover how to nurture each fruit, from understanding their unique seasonal needs to creating the perfect environment with just the right light, soil, and care. Depending on the size of your greenhouse, some options are not ideal to work with.

——Fruit Bushes——

Blackberry, Raspberry, Boysenberry

Fruiting Season: These three fruits are very similar in how they are grown and typically fruit from mid-summer to early fall, with some varieties producing multiple crops throughout the season.

Size: These berry plants can vary in size depending on the variety, ranging from compact dwarf cultivars suitable for containers to sprawling types that require more space.

Light: All three thrive in full sun, requiring at least 6–8 hours of direct sunlight daily for optimal fruit production. In a greenhouse, ensure they receive ample light either naturally or supplemented with grow lights.

Soil: Well-draining, slightly acidic soil with a pH level between 5.5 and 6.5 is ideal for blackberries. A mix of loamy soil with added compost or organic matter helps maintain moisture and fertility.

Watering: Blackberries prefer consistently moist soil, especially during fruiting. Water deeply but infrequently to encourage deep root growth, and avoid overhead watering to prevent fungal diseases.

Temperature: Blackberries thrive in moderate temperatures between 60–75°F (15–24°C) during the growing season. They can tolerate brief periods of colder temperatures but may need protection in colder climates.

Humidity: Moderate humidity levels are suitable for blackberries. Greenhouses provide a controlled environment where humidity can be adjusted as needed to prevent fungal issues.

Maintenance: Regular pruning is essential to maintain each of these plants. Prune out old cane branches after fruiting and thin out new growth to improve air circulation. Trellising or supporting canes helps manage growth and makes harvesting easier.

Blueberry

Fruiting Season: Blueberries typically fruit in summer, with some varieties extending into early fall.

Size: Blueberry bushes range in size from compact dwarf varieties suitable for containers to larger bushes that require space for growth.

Light: Blueberries thrive in full sun to partial shade, requiring at least 6 hours of direct sunlight daily for optimal fruit production. In a greenhouse, provide ample light through natural or supplemental means.

Soil: Well-draining, acidic soil with a pH level between 4.5 and 5.5 is essential for blueberries. Adding peat moss or pine bark mulch to the soil improves acidity and moisture retention.

Watering: Blueberries prefer consistently moist but well-drained soil. Water regularly, especially during dry spells, and mulch around plants to retain moisture and regulate soil temperature.

Temperature: Blueberries thrive in cooler climates and prefer temperatures between 35–85°F (1–29°C) during the growing season. They require chilling hours in winter to set fruit properly.

Humidity: Blueberries prefer moderate humidity levels. Greenhouses provide a controlled environment where humidity can be adjusted to prevent fungal diseases.

Maintenance: Prune blueberry bushes annually to remove dead or diseased wood and encourage new growth. Mulch around plants and protect them from birds with netting during fruiting season.

Cucumber

Fruiting Season: Cucumbers are warm-season crops that typically produce fruit from mid-summer to early fall, depending on the variety.

Size: Cucumber plants can vary in size from compact bush varieties suitable for containers to vining types that require trellises or support.

Light: Cucumbers thrive in full sun, requiring at least 6–8 hours of direct sunlight daily for optimal growth and fruit production. In a greenhouse, provide ample light through natural or supplemental means like grow lights.

Soil: Well-draining, fertile soil with a pH level between 6.0 and 7.0 is ideal for cucumbers. Adding organic matter, such as compost or aged manure, helps improve soil structure and fertility.

Watering: Cucumbers prefer consistently moist soil, especially during flowering and fruiting. Water deeply and regularly, ensuring the soil does not dry out completely between waterings.

Temperature: Cucumbers prefer warm temperatures between 70–85°F (21–29°C) during the growing season. They are sensitive to frost and thrive in a controlled environment provided by a greenhouse.

Humidity: Cucumbers prefer moderate humidity levels. Greenhouses offer a controlled environment where humidity can be adjusted to prevent issues like powdery mildew.

Maintenance: Prune cucumber plants to improve air circulation and reduce the risk of disease. Trellising vining varieties helps save space and keeps fruits off the ground, promoting cleaner, healthier fruit development.

Grape

Fruiting Season: Grapes typically fruit in late summer to early fall, depending on the variety.

Size: Grapevines vary in size from compact varieties suitable for containers to large vines that need support structures like trellises or arbors.

Light: Grapes thrive in full sun, requiring at least 6–8 hours of direct sunlight daily for optimal fruit production. In a greenhouse, provide adequate light through natural or supplemental means.

Soil: Well-draining, fertile soil with a pH level between 5.5 and 7.0 is ideal for grapes. Adding compost or aged manure improves soil fertility and structure.

Watering: Grapes prefer moderately moist soil, especially during fruit development. Water deeply and infrequently, allowing the soil to dry slightly between waterings to prevent root rot.

Temperature: Grapes prefer warm temperatures between 60–75°F (15–24°C) during the growing season. They need a period of winter dormancy with cool temperatures to set fruit properly.

Humidity: Grapes prefer moderate humidity levels. Greenhouses provide a controlled environment where humidity can be managed to prevent diseases like powdery mildew.

Maintenance: Prune grapevines annually in late winter to remove old wood and encourage new growth. Train vines along trellises and thin out fruit clusters to improve air circulation and grape quality.

Peppers

Fruiting Season: Peppers are warm-season crops that produce fruit from mid-summer to fall, depending on the variety and growing conditions.

Size: Pepper plants range from compact varieties suitable for containers to larger plants that may require staking or support.

Light: Peppers thrive in full sun, requiring at least 6–8 hours of direct sunlight daily for optimal growth and fruiting.

Soil: Well-draining, fertile soil with a pH level between 6.0 and 7.0 is ideal for peppers. Amending soil with compost or well-rotted manure provides necessary nutrients and improves soil structure.

Watering: Peppers prefer moderately moist soil. Water deeply and regularly, allowing the soil to dry out slightly between waterings to avoid waterlogged conditions.

Temperature: Peppers prefer warm temperatures between 70–85°F (21–29°C) during the growing season. They are sensitive to cold and benefit from the warmth provided by a greenhouse environment.

Humidity: Peppers prefer moderate humidity levels. Greenhouses allow for humidity control, which helps prevent diseases like blossom end rot.

Maintenance: Prune pepper plants to improve air circulation and remove dead or diseased foliage. Support larger plants with stakes or cages to prevent breakage under the weight of fruit.

Pineapple

Fruiting Season: Pineapples take about 18–24 months to fruit after planting the crown. Once established, they can produce fruit year-round under suitable conditions.

Size: Pineapple plants are compact and can be grown in containers. They typically reach 2–3 feet in height with a spread of 3–4 feet.

Light: Pineapples thrive in full sun, requiring at least 6–8 hours of direct sunlight daily for optimal growth and fruit production. In a greenhouse, ensure they receive ample light through natural or artificial means.

Soil: Well-draining, slightly acidic soil with a pH level between 5.5 and 6.5 is ideal for pineapples. Use a mix of potting soil and perlite or sand to ensure good drainage.

Watering: Pineapples prefer moderately moist soil. Water deeply but infrequently, allowing the soil to dry out slightly between waterings to prevent root rot.

Temperature: Pineapples prefer warm temperatures between 65–95°F (18–35°C). They can tolerate slightly cooler temperatures but should be protected from frost.

Humidity: Pineapples prefer high humidity levels. Greenhouses provide a controlled environment where humidity can be maintained around 50–70% to promote healthy growth.

Maintenance: Maintain consistent moisture levels and provide balanced fertilizer every 2–3 months during the growing season. Protect plants from pests like mealybugs and scale insects.

Strawberry

Fruiting Season: Strawberries typically fruit in spring to early summer, with some varieties producing throughout the summer.

Size: Strawberry plants vary from compact varieties suitable for containers to runners that spread and require space for growth.

Light: Strawberries require full sun for optimal fruiting, though they can tolerate partial shade. In a greenhouse, ensure they receive adequate light through natural or supplemental means.

Soil: Well-draining, fertile soil with a pH level between 5.5 and 6.5 is ideal for strawberries. Incorporating compost or organic matter improves soil structure and nutrient content.

Watering: Strawberries prefer consistently moist soil, especially during fruit development. Water regularly, keeping the soil evenly moist but not waterlogged, to prevent fruit rot.

Temperature: Strawberries prefer cool temperatures between 60–75°F (15–24°C) during the growing season. They may benefit from protection in hot climates to prevent heat stress.

Humidity: Moderate humidity levels are suitable for strawberries. Greenhouses provide a controlled environment where humidity can be regulated to prevent fungal diseases.

Maintenance: Trim runners regularly to promote larger fruit production and prevent overcrowding. Mulch around plants to retain moisture and suppress weeds, and cover with netting to protect from birds.

Tomato

Fruiting Season: Tomatoes are warm-season crops that produce fruit from mid-summer to fall, depending on the variety and growing conditions.

Size: Tomato plants vary from compact determinate varieties suitable for containers to sprawling indeterminate types that may require staking or trellising.

Light: Tomatoes thrive in full sun, requiring at least 6–8 hours of direct sunlight daily for optimal growth and fruiting. Provide ample light through natural or supplemental means like grow lights.

Soil: Well-draining, fertile soil with a pH level between 6.0 and 6.8 is ideal for tomatoes. Amend soil with compost or well-rotted manure before planting to ensure good soil structure and fertility.

Watering: Tomatoes prefer consistently moist soil. Water deeply and regularly, aiming to keep the soil evenly moist but not waterlogged to prevent diseases like blossom end rot.

Temperature: Tomatoes prefer warm temperatures between 70–85°F (21–29°C) during the growing season. They are sensitive to frost and benefit from the warmth provided by a greenhouse.

Humidity: Tomatoes prefer moderate humidity levels. Greenhouses provide a controlled environment where humidity can be adjusted to prevent diseases like powdery mildew.

Maintenance: Prune tomato plants to improve air circulation and remove suckers. Support indeterminate varieties with stakes or trellises to keep fruits off the ground and reduce the risk of disease.

——Fruit Trees——

Apple

Fruiting Season: Apples typically fruit in late summer to early fall, with harvest time varying by variety.

Size: Apple trees range in size from dwarf varieties suitable for containers to standard trees that require space for growth. Most other sizes are too large for most easily accessible greenhouses.

Light: Apples thrive in full sun, requiring at least 6–8 hours of direct sunlight daily for optimal fruit production. In a greenhouse, ensure they receive adequate light through natural or supplemental means.

Soil: Well-draining, fertile soil with a pH level between 6.0 and 7.0 is ideal for apples. Incorporating compost or well-rotted manure improves soil fertility and structure.

Watering: Apples prefer moderately moist soil, especially during fruit development. Water deeply and infrequently, allowing the soil to dry slightly between waterings to prevent root rot.

Temperature: Apples prefer cool to moderate temperatures between 60–75°F (15–24°C) during the growing season. They require a period of winter chilling hours to set fruit properly.

Humidity: Apples prefer moderate humidity levels. Greenhouses provide a controlled environment where humidity can be managed to prevent diseases like apple scab.

Maintenance: Prune apple trees annually in late winter to remove dead or diseased wood and shape the tree for better fruit production. Thin out fruit clusters to promote larger, healthier apples.

Avocado

Fruiting Season: Avocados can produce fruit year-round in suitable climates. Flowering and fruiting times may vary depending on the variety and growing conditions.

Size: Avocado trees are large, typically reaching heights of 30–40 feet when grown outdoors. Dwarf varieties suitable for containers are available.

Light: Avocados thrive in full sun, requiring at least 6–8 hours of direct sunlight daily for optimal growth and fruiting. In a greenhouse, provide ample light through natural or supplemental means like grow lights.

Soil: Well-draining, slightly acidic soil with a pH level between 6.0 and 6.5 is ideal for avocados. Use a mix of potting soil and perlite or sand to ensure good drainage.

Watering: Avocados prefer consistently moist soil. Water deeply but infrequently, allowing the soil to dry out slightly between waterings to avoid waterlogged conditions.

Temperature: Avocados prefer warm temperatures between 60–85°F (16–29°C) and are sensitive to frost. They benefit from the warmth and protection provided by a greenhouse.

Humidity: Avocados prefer moderate to high humidity levels. Greenhouses allow for humidity control, which helps promote healthy growth and fruit production.

Maintenance: Prune avocado trees annually in late winter to shape the tree and remove dead or damaged branches. Fertilize regularly with a balanced fertilizer formulated for fruit trees.

Banana

Fruiting Season: Bananas can fruit year-round in tropical climates. The exact season can vary depending on the variety and growing conditions.

Size: Banana plants are large herbaceous plants that can reach heights of 10–30 feet or more, depending on the variety and growing conditions.

Light: Bananas thrive in full sun to partial shade, requiring at least 6–8 hours of direct sunlight daily for optimal growth and fruiting. In a greenhouse, provide bright, filtered light to mimic their natural habitat.

Soil: Well-draining, fertile soil with organic matter is ideal for bananas. Soil pH should be around 5.5–6.5. Regularly amend soil with compost or well-rotted manure.

Watering: Bananas require consistently moist soil. Water deeply and regularly, especially during dry periods, to keep the soil evenly moist but not waterlogged.

Temperature: Bananas prefer warm temperatures between 75–85°F (24–29°C) during the day and above 60°F (15°C) at night. They are sensitive to frost and thrive in the warmth of a greenhouse.

Humidity: Bananas prefer high humidity levels, around 50–70%. Greenhouses can provide a humid environment, especially in drier climates.

Maintenance: Prune banana plants to remove old leaves and suckers to encourage healthy growth and fruit production. Fertilize regularly with a balanced fertilizer to provide necessary nutrients.

Citrus (Lemon, Lime, Orange)

Fruiting Season: Citrus fruits generally ripen in late fall through winter, depending on the variety. Some varieties may produce fruit year-round in ideal conditions.

Size: Citrus trees vary in size depending on the variety and rootstock. Dwarf varieties are suitable for containers, reaching heights of 6–10 feet, while standard trees can grow much larger.

Light: Citrus trees thrive in full sun, requiring at least 6–8 hours of direct sunlight daily for optimal growth and fruiting. In a greenhouse, ensure they receive bright light through natural or supplemental means.

Soil: Well-draining, slightly acidic soil with a pH level between 5.5 and 6.5 is ideal for citrus. Use a potting mix formulated for citrus trees or amend garden soil with compost and sand for better drainage.

Watering: Citrus trees prefer consistently moist soil. Water deeply and allow the soil to dry slightly between waterings. Avoid overwatering to prevent root rot.

Temperature: Citrus trees prefer warm temperatures between 55–85°F (13–29°C) and are sensitive to frost. They benefit from the warmth and protection provided by a greenhouse.

Humidity: Citrus trees prefer moderate humidity levels. Greenhouses allow for humidity control, which helps prevent issues like leaf drop and fruit splitting.

Maintenance: Prune citrus trees annually to remove dead or crossing branches and improve air circulation. Fertilize regularly with a citrus-specific fertilizer to promote healthy growth and fruit production.

Fig

Fruiting Season: Figs produce two crops annually: an early crop in early summer on last year's wood and a main crop in late summer or early fall on the current year's growth.

Size: Fig trees can range from small to medium-sized, depending on the variety and growing conditions. They can be trained to grow in containers or as large bushes or trees.

Light: Figs thrive in full sun, requiring at least 6–8 hours of direct sunlight daily for optimal growth and fruiting. In a greenhouse, ensure they receive ample light through natural or supplemental means.

Soil: Well-draining, loamy soil with a pH level between 6.0 and 6.5 is ideal for figs. Amend soil with compost or aged manure to improve fertility and drainage.

Watering: Figs prefer moderately moist soil. Water deeply during dry periods, allowing the soil to dry out slightly between waterings. Avoid overwatering, especially in containers.

Temperature: Figs prefer warm temperatures between 75–85°F (24–29°C) during the growing season. They are hardy to USDA zones 7–11 but benefit from the warmth of a greenhouse in cooler climates.

Humidity: Figs prefer moderate humidity levels. Greenhouses provide a controlled environment where humidity can be adjusted to prevent issues like fruit drop.

Maintenance: Prune fig trees in late winter to early spring to remove dead or diseased wood and shape the tree. Fertilize with a balanced fertilizer in early spring and midsummer to promote fruiting.

Guava

Fruiting Season: Guavas can produce fruit year-round in tropical climates. The main fruiting season is typically in late summer to fall.

Size: Guava trees vary in size from small shrubs to large trees, depending on the variety. Dwarf varieties are suitable for containers, reaching heights of 3–6 feet.

Light: Guavas thrive in full sun to partial shade, requiring at least 4–6 hours of direct sunlight daily for optimal growth and fruiting. In a greenhouse, provide bright, filtered light.

Soil: Well-draining, fertile soil with a pH level between 5.5 and 7.0 is ideal for guavas. Amend soil with compost or well-rotted manure to improve fertility and drainage.

Watering: Guavas prefer consistently moist soil. Water deeply during dry periods, allowing the soil to dry slightly between waterings. Reduce watering in winter when growth slows.

Temperature: Guavas prefer warm temperatures between 70–85°F (21–29°C) and are sensitive to frost. They benefit from the warmth and protection provided by a greenhouse.

Humidity: Guavas prefer moderate humidity levels. Greenhouses can provide a humid environment, especially in drier climates.

Maintenance: Prune guava trees annually after fruiting to remove dead or crowded branches and improve air circulation. Fertilize with a balanced fertilizer formulated for fruit trees.

Papaya

Fruiting Season: Papayas can produce fruit year-round in tropical climates. The exact fruiting season may vary depending on the variety and growing conditions.

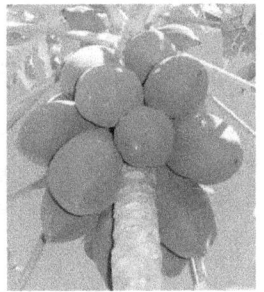

Size: Papaya trees are relatively fast-growing and can reach heights of 10–30 feet, depending on the variety. Dwarf varieties are available for containers.

Light: Papayas thrive in full sun, requiring at least 6–8 hours of direct sunlight daily for optimal growth and fruiting. In a greenhouse, provide bright light with some shade during the hottest part of the day.

Soil: Well-draining, fertile soil with a pH level between 5.5 and 7.0 is ideal for papayas. Amend soil with compost or aged manure to improve fertility and drainage.

Watering: Papayas prefer consistently moist soil. Water deeply and regularly, especially during dry periods, to keep the soil evenly moist but not waterlogged.

Temperature: Papayas prefer warm temperatures between 70–90°F (21–32°C) and are sensitive to frost. They benefit from the warmth and protection provided by a greenhouse.

Humidity: Papayas prefer moderate humidity levels. Greenhouses provide a controlled environment where humidity can be adjusted to promote healthy growth.

Maintenance: Prune papaya trees to remove dead or damaged leaves and fruiting stems. Fertilize regularly with a balanced fertilizer formulated for fruiting plants to support growth and fruit production.

Soursop

Fruiting Season: Soursops typically fruit in late summer to fall, depending on the variety and growing conditions. Some varieties may produce fruit year-round in tropical climates.

Size: Soursop trees can reach heights of 20–30 feet or more, depending on the variety and growing conditions.

Light: Soursops thrive in full sun, requiring at least 6–8 hours of direct sunlight daily for optimal growth and fruiting. In a greenhouse, provide bright light with some shade during the hottest part of the day.

Soil: Well-draining, fertile soil with a pH level between 5.5 and 6.5 is ideal for soursops. Amend soil with compost or well-rotted manure to improve fertility and drainage.

Watering: Soursops prefer consistently moist soil. Water deeply and regularly, especially during dry periods, to keep the soil evenly moist but not waterlogged.

Temperature: Soursops prefer warm temperatures between 75–85°F (24–29°C) and are sensitive to frost. They benefit from the warmth and protection provided by a greenhouse.

Humidity: Soursops prefer moderate humidity levels. Greenhouses provide a controlled environment where humidity can be adjusted to promote healthy growth and fruit production.

Maintenance: Prune soursop trees to remove dead or damaged branches and improve air circulation. Fertilize regularly with a balanced fertilizer formulated for fruit trees to support growth and fruiting.

Chapter Five

Protect Your Garden from Weeds, Diseases, and Pests

HAVE YOU EVER HAD one of those moments where life gets busy, and you realize you've neglected something important? That's exactly what happened to me with my indoor garden. I got so caught up in daily life that I didn't notice the weeds creeping in, pests making themselves at home, and diseases quietly spreading among my beloved plants.

It wasn't until the issues became glaringly obvious—like a jungle of weeds and leaves turning yellow—that I snapped back to attention. But the good news is I learned how to tackle these challenges head-on and reclaim my garden. Here are great ways protect your garden from these sneaky intruders and keep it thriving all year round.

Section 1: Weed Control in Indoor Gardens

Weed control in indoor gardens is crucial for maintaining a healthy and productive growing space. By understanding the dangers of chemical weed killers and learning how weeds spread, you can take proactive steps to manage them effectively.

The Dangers of Chemical Weed Killers & Pesticides

Chemical weed killers and pesticides might seem like a quick fix, but they come with significant downsides. These chemicals don't just target weeds; they can also harm beneficial insects, pets, and even people.

Over time, the chemicals can seep into the soil, contaminating it and potentially affecting the plants you're trying to protect. They can spread from one plant to another, posing a risk to your entire garden.

Additionally, chemical residues can linger on fruits and vegetables, making them unsafe for consumption. The dangers extend beyond your indoor garden as well.

These chemicals can be washed away by water, entering local water systems and impacting wildlife and ecosystems. It's essential to be mindful of these risks when considering weed control methods.

How Weeds Spread in Greenhouses

Weeds are tenacious and can find their way into your greenhouse through various means. They can hitch a ride on your shoes, clothing, or gardening tools. They can also enter through open windows, vents, or even be carried in by the wind.

Once inside, weeds can quickly take root in the soil and spread. They thrive in the warm, humid conditions of a greenhouse, making it important to stay vigilant and take preventative measures. Regularly inspecting your greenhouse and keeping it clean can help prevent weeds from establishing a foothold.

Managing Weeds Organically

Effective weed management in a greenhouse involves a combination of prevention and control methods. Start by keeping your greenhouse clean and free of debris where weeds can hide.

Regularly inspect your plants and soil for signs of weeds. When you spot them, remove them promptly, making sure to get the roots to prevent regrowth. Mulching can also be an effective way to suppress weed growth.

Organic mulches like straw or wood chips can create a barrier that prevents weeds from getting the sunlight they need to grow.

Additionally, practicing good garden hygiene, such as disinfecting tools and wearing clean shoes, can help keep weeds at bay.

Homemade Weed Killers

If you're looking for an eco-friendly and safe way to tackle weeds, homemade weed killers can be an excellent solution. These homemade solutions are not only effective but also safe for your plants, pets, and the environment.

By using these natural alternatives, you can keep your indoor garden weed-free without resorting to harmful chemicals. Here are a few recipes you can try.

Vinegar and Salt Solution

Mix 1 gallon of white vinegar with 1 cup of salt and 1 tablespoon of dish soap. Pour the mixture into a spray bottle and apply it directly to the weeds.

The vinegar will dry out the weeds, while the salt prevents them from growing back. Be careful to avoid spraying this solution on your desirable plants, as it can harm them too.

Boiling Water

Sometimes, the simplest solutions are the best. Pouring boiling water directly onto weeds can kill them almost instantly. This method is especially effective for weeds growing in cracks and crevices. It's safe, chemical-free, and can be used as often as needed.

Lemon Juice Spray

Combine 1 cup of lemon juice with 1 quart of white vinegar. The acidity of the lemon juice, combined with the vinegar, makes this a powerful weed killer.

Spray the mixture directly onto the weeds, and they should start to wilt within a few hours.

Corn Gluten Meal

This is an organic pre-emergent weed killer that prevents weed seeds from germinating. It's safe for pets and also adds nitrogen to the soil, which can benefit your plants.

Soap and Water Solution

Mix 2 tablespoons of liquid dish soap with 1 quart of water. Spray this solution directly onto the weeds. The soap breaks down the weed's outer layer, causing it to dehydrate and die.

Baking Soda

Sprinkle baking soda directly onto the weeds. This works well for weeds growing in cracks and crevices. The baking soda increases the salt content in the soil, which weeds can't tolerate.

Section 2: Disease Prevention and Treatment

Disease prevention and treatment in indoor gardens require vigilance, proper care, and timely intervention. By understanding common diseases, adopting preventative measures, and using effective detection and treatments, you can maintain a healthy and thriving indoor garden.

Remember, the key is to create an environment that supports plant health while minimizing conditions that favor disease development.

Common Plant Diseases in Greenhouses

Greenhouses create a controlled environment ideal for growing plants, but they also provide perfect conditions for various plant diseases to thrive. Understanding these common diseases is crucial for maintaining a healthy indoor garden.

Powdery Mildew

This is one of the most prevalent greenhouse diseases. It appears as a white, powdery substance on the surfaces of leaves, stems, and buds. Powdery mildew thrives in warm, dry conditions, often  spreading rapidly if left unchecked. It can stunt plant growth and reduce yields.

Botrytis Blight (Gray Mold)

Botrytis blight, or gray mold, is another common problem in greenhouses. It manifests as gray, fuzzy mold on leaves, flowers, and fruit. High humidity and poor ventilation exacerbate this disease. Botrytis blight can lead to extensive plant damage if not controlled early.

Root Rot

Root rot is often caused by overwatering and poorly drained soils. It leads to brown, mushy roots and wilting plants, even when soil moisture seems adequate. Root rot 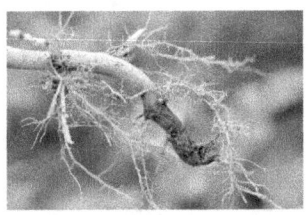 can be tricky because it affects the plant below the soil surface, making early detection difficult.

Leaf Spot Diseases

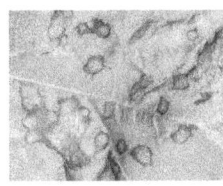

Various fungal and bacterial pathogens cause leaf spots, which appear as discolored spots on leaves. These spots can be yellow, brown, or black and may have a halo or border. Leaf spots often occur in humid conditions and can weaken plants by reducing their photosynthetic capacity.

Damping-Off Disease

This disease primarily affects seedlings, causing them to rot at the soil line and collapse. Damping-off is caused by several soilborne fungi and is favored by cool, wet conditions.

Fusarium Wilt

Fusarium wilt is a soilborne disease that causes yellowing and wilting of leaves, often affecting one side of the plant first. It clogs the plant's vascular system, preventing water and nutrients from reaching the leaves. There is no cure for fusarium wilt, so prevention is crucial.

Downy Mildew

Downy mildew appears as yellow or white patches on the upper surfaces of leaves, with a corresponding downy growth on the undersides. It thrives in cool, moist conditions.

Disease Prevention Strategies

Keeping your greenhouse plants healthy and disease-free involves proactive measures and vigilant care. Implementing effective disease prevention strategies ensures that your plants thrive in a controlled environment. Here are some essential strategies to keep your greenhouse disease-free.

Maintain Cleanliness

One of the most critical steps in preventing plant diseases is maintaining a clean greenhouse. Remove plant debris, dead leaves, and weeds regularly as they can harbor pathogens.

Disinfect tools, pots, and benches frequently to prevent the spread of diseases. Use a mild bleach solution or commercial disinfectants to clean surfaces and equipment.

Control Humidity

High humidity levels create ideal conditions for many fungal and bacterial diseases. Use fans and vents to improve air circulation and reduce humidity.

Dehumidifiers can also be effective in maintaining optimal humidity levels. Water plants early in the day so that any excess moisture evaporates quickly, reducing the risk of disease.

Ensure Proper Watering

Overwatering is a common cause of plant diseases, especially root rot and fungal infections. Water plants at their base to keep foliage dry, and ensure pots have adequate drainage to prevent waterlogging.

Using drip irrigation systems can help deliver water directly to the roots while keeping the leaves dry.

Grow Disease-Resistant Varieties

Choosing disease-resistant plant varieties is a practical way to reduce the risk of infections. Many seed catalogs and nurseries offer varieties bred for resistance to common greenhouse diseases.

Incorporating these plants into your garden can significantly lower the chances of disease outbreaks.

Provide Adequate Spacing

Overcrowding plants can impede air circulation and create a humid micro-environment conducive to disease development.

Ensure adequate spacing between plants to promote airflow and reduce humidity around the foliage. Proper spacing also allows you to monitor and manage each plant more effectively.

Follow Healthy Soil Practices

Using sterile, high-quality soil is important to prevent soilborne diseases. Avoid reusing old soil, as it may contain pathogens. Incorporate organic matter to improve soil structure and drainage.

Monitor and Inspect Regularly

Regularly inspect plants for early signs of disease. Look for discoloration, spots, mold, or wilting. Early detection allows for prompt action, such as removing infected plants or applying appropriate treatments. Using magnifying glasses can help identify tiny pests and early disease symptoms.

Ensure Ventilation

Good ventilation is important in preventing diseases caused by excess humidity. Use fans to create a gentle breeze and open vents to allow fresh air to circulate. This helps maintain a dry environment that is less favorable for disease development.

Sanitize Seeds and Cuttings

Diseases can be introduced through seeds and cuttings. Treat seeds with hot water or fungicides before planting. Ensure cuttings are taken from healthy, disease-free plants and use clean, sterilized tools to make cuts.

Implement Crop Rotation

Crop rotation is not just for outdoor gardens; it can be beneficial in greenhouses too. Rotating crops helps break the life cycles of soilborne pathogens and reduces the likelihood of disease recurrence.

Avoid planting the same family of plants in the same location year after year.

Allow Biological Controls

Introduce beneficial organisms that can help control disease-causing pathogens. Mycorrhizal fungi, beneficial bacteria, and nematodes can enhance soil health and suppress harmful microbes.

These biological controls can be integrated into your gardening routine to create a balanced and resilient ecosystem.

Organic Treatments

Use organic treatments and homemade remedies to manage diseases. Neem oil, baking soda solutions, and compost teas can help control fungal infections and boost plant immunity.

These treatments are eco-friendly and reduce reliance on chemical pesticides.

Detecting Diseases Early

Early detection of plant diseases is vital for effective management. Regularly check your plants for any unusual signs, such as discolored leaves, spots, wilting, or stunted growth. In addition to visual inspections, you can use technology to help detect diseases early.

Humidity sensors can alert you to conditions that might promote fungal growth, while soil moisture meters can help you avoid overwatering. Some advanced tools even use artificial intelligence to analyze plant health and detect diseases at an early stage. By staying vigilant and utilizing available tools, you can catch problems early and take action before they spread.

Natural Fungicides and Mold Control

Controlling fungal infections and mold in your greenhouse can be achieved using natural fungicides and mold control methods. These eco-friendly solutions are effective and safe for both plants and the environment. Here are some natural options to consider.

Neem Oil

Neem oil is a versatile and potent natural fungicide. It works by disrupting the life cycle of fungi, preventing spore germination and growth. Mix 1 teaspoon of neem oil and 1/4 teaspoon of dish soap in water. Then spray the solution on affected plants. Neem oil is effective against powdery mildew, rust, and black spot.

Baking Soda Solution

Mix 1 tablespoon of baking soda with a gallon of water and add a few drops of dish soap to help the solution adhere to the leaves.

Baking soda is a simple yet effective remedy for fungal infections. This mixture helps create an alkaline environment on plant surfaces, inhibiting fungal growth.

Garlic Extract

Crush several cloves of garlic and steep them in water for 24 hours. Strain the mixture and use it as a spray on plants affected by fungal infections.

Garlic has natural antifungal properties. Garlic extract can help combat powdery mildew, downy mildew, and other fungal diseases.

Milk Spray

Mix 1 part milk with 9 parts water and spray the solution on affected plants.

Milk, particularly skim milk, can help control powdery mildew. The proteins in milk can help inhibit the growth of fungal spores. Apply this solution weekly for best results.

Horticultural Oils

Mix the oil with water according to the manufacturer's instructions and spray it on affected plants.

Horticultural oils, such as mineral oil or dormant oil, can effectively control fungal diseases and molds. These oils work by smothering fungal spores and disrupting their development.

Cinnamon

Sprinkle ground cinnamon around the base of plants or dust it directly on affected areas. Cinnamon is a natural antifungal agent. Cinnamon can help prevent and control mold and fungal infections in seedlings and mature plants.

Vinegar Solution

Mix 1 part vinegar with 3 parts water and spray the solution on the infected areas.

White vinegar can be used to control mold and fungal growth. Vinegar's acetic acid content helps kill mold spores and prevent their spread.

Hydrogen Peroxide

Mix 1 part hydrogen peroxide with 10 parts water and use it as a spray on plants and soil.

Hydrogen peroxide is an excellent mold control agent. Hydrogen peroxide helps kill mold spores and can improve soil aeration.

Sulfur

Sulfur is a traditional and effective natural fungicide. It can be applied as a dust or mixed with water to create a spray. Sulfur helps control a wide range of fungal diseases, including powdery mildew and rust. Use sulfur in well-ventilated areas to avoid inhaling the dust.

Resolving Plant Diseases

If your plants do become sick, it's important to act quickly to rehabilitate them. Start by isolating the affected plants to prevent the disease from spreading to healthy ones. Trim off any diseased or dead parts of the plant.

For root rot, you may need to repot the plant in fresh, sterile soil and ensure better drainage. Adjusting watering practices and improving air circulation can help the plant recover. In some cases, you might need to use an organic fungicide or insecticide to combat the disease.

Be patient and consistent with your care, and your plants can often recover from even severe infections. Regular monitoring and timely intervention are key to resolving plant diseases effectively.

Section 3: Common Indoor Pests

Indoor gardening offers a controlled environment that can be inviting not only to plants but also to various pests seeking shelter and food sources. Understanding and managing common indoor pests is crucial for maintaining plant health and productivity. Here are some of the most prevalent indoor pests and strategies to control them.

Aphids

Aphids are small, soft-bodied insects that feed on plant sap, causing leaves to curl, yellow, and distort. They reproduce quickly, making early detection and intervention essential. To control aphids, spray affected  plants with a strong stream of water to dislodge them. Alternatively, use insecticidal soap or neem oil, which suffocates aphids without harming plants.

Spider Mites

Spider mites are tiny garden pests that thrive in warm, dry conditions. They pierce plant cells and feed on sap. This causes stippling, yellowing, and webbing on the leaves. Increase humidity levels to deter spider mites, as they prefer dry environments. Use insecticidal soap or neem oil to control infestations, ensuring thorough coverage of both sides of leaves.

Whiteflies

Whiteflies are small, moth-like insects that cluster on the undersides of leaves. They suck sap from plants, causing leaves to yellow, wilt, and distort. Yellow sticky traps can help monitor and reduce whitefly populations. Vacuuming affected plants with a handheld vacuum can also provide immediate relief. For severe infestations, use insecticidal soap or neem oil.

Mealybugs

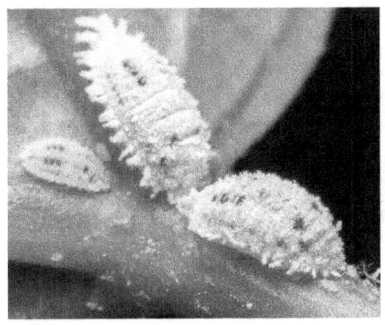

Mealybugs are small, cotton-like pests that feed on plant sap and excrete honeydew, attracting ants and promoting mold growth. Remove mealybugs by dabbing them with a cotton swab dipped in rubbing alcohol or insecticidal soap. Prune heavily infested plant parts and isolate affected plants to prevent spread.

Fungus Gnats

Fungus gnats are small, mosquito-like insects that lay eggs in moist soil. Larvae feed on plant roots, causing stunted growth and yellowing leaves.

Allow soil to dry between waterings to deter fungus gnat larvae. Use yellow sticky traps to monitor adult populations and reduce numbers. Applying a soil drench of neem oil or beneficial nematodes can effectively control larvae.

Scale Insects

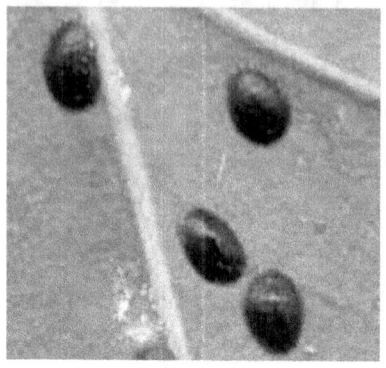

Scale insects appear as small, waxy bumps on stems and leaves, feeding on plant sap and weakening the plant over time. Remove scales by gently scraping them off with a soft brush or cloth soaked in rubbing alcohol.

Prune heavily infested plant parts and treat with insecticidal soap or horticultural oil for persistent infestations.

Thrips

Thrips are tiny, slender insects that feed on plant tissues, causing stippling, discoloration, and distorted growth. Monitor thrips with yellow sticky traps placed near plants. Prune and dispose of heavily infested plant parts.

Use insecticidal soap or neem oil to control thrips effectively.

Snails and Slugs

Snails and slugs are nocturnal pests that chew on plant leaves and stems, leaving behind slime trails. Remove them by hand during evening hours or early morning. Create barriers using copper tape or diatomaceous earth around plant containers to deter them.

Small Animals

Small creatures such as mice and rabbits, can find their way into greenhouses seeking shelter and food. Use physical barriers, such as wire mesh or hardware cloth, to prevent access to greenhouse openings.

Remove food sources and keep the greenhouse environment clean and free of debris that can attract rodents.

Birds

Birds may enter greenhouses in search of shelter or food, causing damage to plants and creating sanitation issues. Install bird netting or mesh over greenhouse openings to prevent entry. Consider using reflective objects or bird scare devices to deter birds from landing and nesting in the greenhouse.

Spices and Herbs as Pest Control

Using spices and herbs for pest control in your garden is a natural and sustainable approach that can effectively deter insects and protect your plants. Here's how you can harness the power of spices and herbs to keep pests at bay.

Cayenne Pepper

Cayenne pepper and other hot spices like chili powder and paprika are effective deterrents for pests, such as ants, aphids, and caterpillars. Sprinkle these spices around the base of plants or create a spray by mixing them with water and a small amount of dish soap to adhere to plant surfaces.

Cinnamon

Cinnamon has antifungal properties and can also deter ants, gnats, and other pests from invading your plants. Dust cinnamon powder around plant stems and on the soil surface to create a barrier that pests find unappealing.

Garlic

Garlic is a potent insect repellent due to its strong odor. Crush fresh garlic cloves and steep them in water overnight to create a garlic spray. Strain the mixture and spray it on plant leaves to deter aphids, spider mites, and whiteflies.

Basil

Basil repels mosquitoes, flies, and aphids with its strong aroma. Plant basil near susceptible plants or use it as a border plant to discourage pests from entering your garden. You can also make a basil tea spray by steeping fresh basil leaves in hot water and spraying it on plants.

Rosemary

Rosemary is effective against cabbage moths, carrot flies, and mosquitoes. Place sprigs of fresh rosemary around garden beds or steep rosemary leaves in water to create a spray. Rosemary oil can also be diluted and applied to plant foliage to deter pests.

Mint

Mint repels ants, aphids, and cabbage moths. Plant mint in pots near garden entrances or infested areas to discourage pests. Crush fresh mint leaves and scatter them around plants, or steep them in water to create a mint spray for application.

Creating Homemade Insecticides

Creating homemade insecticides can be a practical and eco-friendly approach to managing pests in your indoor garden. These DIY solutions often use common household ingredients and are gentler on plants and the environment compared to synthetic chemicals. Here are some effective homemade insecticides you can easily make and use.

Neem Oil Spray

- Mix 1-2 tablespoons of neem oil

- A few drops of mild liquid soap to emulsify the oil

- 1 quart of warm water

Shake well before use and spray directly on affected plants, covering both sides of leaves thoroughly. Neem oil is derived from the seeds of the neem tree and acts as a natural insecticide, repellent, and fungicide. Neem oil disrupts the insect's hormonal balance, inhibiting their ability to feed and reproduce.

Garlic and Pepper Spray

- 2-3 garlic cloves

- 1-2 hot peppers (such as jalapeño or cayenne)

- 1 quart of water

Blend together and let the mixture steep overnight, then strain it through a cheesecloth or fine sieve. Add a few drops of mild liquid soap to help the mixture adhere to plant surfaces. Spray directly on plants, focusing on areas where pests are present. Reapply every few days or after rain. Garlic and hot peppers contain natural compounds that repel and deter many pests.

Soap Spray

- Mix 1-2 teaspoons of mild liquid soap (such as Castile soap or dish soap)

- 1 quart of water

Shake well to ensure the soap is thoroughly mixed. Spray the solution on affected plants, covering both sides of leaves and stems. A soap spray is effective against soft-bodied insects like aphids, spider mites, and whiteflies.

The soap disrupts the insect's cell membranes, causing dehydration and eventual death. Avoid using soap sprays during hot, sunny conditions to prevent potential leaf damage.

Oil Spray

- Mix 1-2 tablespoons of vegetable oil (such as soybean or canola oil)

- 1 quart of water and a few drops of mild liquid soap.

Shake well before use. Spray the mixture on affected plants, ensuring thorough coverage. Oil sprays are effective against aphids, scales, and mites but may cause leaf damage if applied excessively or during hot weather. An oil spray suffocates and repels pests by coating their bodies and blocking their breathing pores.

Herbal Infusions

Steep a handful of fresh or dried herbs (such as mint, basil, or rosemary) in 1 quart of boiling water for several hours. Strain the mixture and add a few drops of mild liquid soap.

Spray the infusion on plants as needed, focusing on areas with pest activity. Herbal infusions not only repel pests but also add a pleasant scent to your indoor garden. Certain herbs have natural insect-repellent properties.

Using Beneficial Plants and Insects

Using beneficial plants and insects is a natural and effective way to manage pests and promote a healthy garden ecosystem. Here's how you can harness the power of beneficial organisms to safeguard your plants.

Companion Plants

Integrate companion plants that attract beneficial insects or repel harmful pests. For example, planting aromatic sage alongside cabbage can ward off cabbage moths, while nasturtiums protect squash from squash bugs.

Pairing tomatoes with basil not only improves flavor but also deters tomato hornworms. Another great combo is marigolds with tomatoes or cucumbers, as marigolds repel nematodes and attract pollinators. Please refer to Chapter 2 for more recommendations and combinations.

Nectar-Rich Flowers

Include nectar-producing flowers, such as cosmos, sunflowers, and zinnias, to attract beneficial insects like predatory wasps and hoverflies. These insects feed on aphids, caterpillars, and other pests, reducing their populations naturally.

Ladybugs

Ladybugs are voracious predators of aphids, scale insects, and mites. Encourage their presence by planting pollen and nectar-rich flowers, and avoid using broad-spectrum pesticides that can harm beneficial insects.

Predatory Wasps

Parasitic wasps and hoverflies prey on aphids, caterpillars, and other soft-bodied pests. Planting dill, fennel, and yarrow attracts these insects, which help control pest populations without harming beneficial species.

Praying Mantises

Praying mantises are generalist predators that feed on a wide range of garden pests, including beetles, moths, and aphids. They are beneficial additions to the garden ecosystem and can be attracted by providing suitable habitat and avoiding insecticides.

Pest-Resistant Greenhouses

Designing a pest-resistant greenhouse involves strategic planning and implementation of physical barriers and preventive measures to minimize pest entry and infestation.

Here are key considerations for designing a pest-resistant greenhouse.

Structure and Ventilation

Start with a sturdy greenhouse structure that seals tightly to prevent pests from entering through gaps or openings. Ensure doors and windows are equipped with tight-fitting screens to keep out insects while allowing adequate ventilation for airflow, which helps maintain plant health and reduces humidity levels that attract pests.

Flooring and Benches

Choose flooring materials that are easy to clean and disinfect, such as concrete or gravel, to eliminate potential pest habitats like weeds or debris. Raised benches for plants can further discourage pests by creating a barrier between soil and plants, reducing the risk of soil-borne pests accessing plant roots.

Screening and Netting

Install fine mesh screens or netting over vents, windows, and doorways to prevent flying insects and larger pests like birds from entering the greenhouse. Mesh size should be small enough to exclude pests while allowing adequate airflow and light penetration.

Quarantine and Sanitation

Establish a quarantine area for new plants or materials entering the greenhouse to prevent introducing pests. Regularly clean and sanitize greenhouse surfaces, tools, and equipment to minimize pest reservoirs and prevent cross-contamination.

Protect Your Garden from Critters

Defending your garden from critters requires a proactive approach that includes both physical barriers and humane deterrent methods. Here's how you can effectively safeguard your garden.

Fencing and Enclosures

Install sturdy fences around your garden perimeter to deter larger animals like deer, rabbits, and raccoons. Use fences with buried mesh to prevent burrowing animals from accessing your garden beds. Consider adding netting or wire mesh enclosures over vulnerable plants or beds to further protect against birds and smaller pests.

Raised Beds and Containers

Planting in raised beds or containers can help deter ground-dwelling pests, such as slugs, snails, and groundhogs.

Raised beds elevate plants above ground level, making them less accessible to crawling pests. Containers placed on elevated surfaces or shelves also discourage pests from reaching plants.

Motion-Activated Devices

Install motion-activated lights, sprinklers, or sound devices that startle, scare, and deter animals when they go near your garden. These devices can effectively deter nocturnal pests like raccoons and deer, as well as smaller animals that are deterred by sudden movements or noises.

Chapter Six

Wintering and Extreme Weather

As the warm days of summer yield to the crisp chill of autumn, gardeners must pivot their focus to safeguarding their precious plants against the harsh embrace of winter. Proper preparation not only protects plants but also sets the stage for a successful transition and thriving growth come spring.

Section 1: Preparing for Winter

Preparing your greenhouse for winter is a proactive investment in the longevity and productivity of your plants. With careful planning and attention to detail, your winterized greenhouse will not only survive but thrive, providing a haven for plants and a rewarding sanctuary for your gardening endeavors.

Understanding Winterization

The winterization process involves preparing plants for the dormant period when external conditions are not conducive to active growth. This process is important for maintaining plant health and ensuring they survive until favorable conditions return.

During winter, plants undergo physiological changes to conserve energy and protect themselves from cold stress, such as slowing down metabolic processes and reducing water content in cells to prevent freezing damage.

Understanding the specific needs of each plant species is important, as winter hardiness varies widely among different types of plants. Winterization, or preparing plants and structures for winter conditions, is crucial for maintaining a healthy greenhouse environment.

This process involves a combination of insulating techniques, adjusting environmental controls, and ensuring plant readiness for cooler temperatures and reduced daylight.

By understanding these basics of wintering, gardeners can effectively prepare their plants for dormancy, ensuring they emerge healthy and vigorous when spring arrives.

Winterization Techniques

Winterization techniques are essential for protecting gardens and greenhouses from the harsh conditions of winter, ensuring plants survive and thrive when warmer weather returns. By implementing these winterization techniques, gardeners can create a resilient environment for their plants, minimizing winter damage and promoting healthier growth come spring.

Insulate Structures

Begin by inspecting the structural integrity of greenhouses and garden structures. Ensure that all windows, doors, and vents are sealed properly to minimize heat loss.

Consider adding additional insulation, such as bubble wrap or thermal curtains, to retain heat inside the greenhouse.

Clean and Maintain Greenhouse

Before winter arrives, thoroughly clean the greenhouse or garden area. Remove any debris, dead plants, and weeds that can harbor pests and diseases over winter.

Cleaning also includes sanitizing tools and equipment to prevent the spread of pathogens.

Mulch and Protect Soil

Apply a thick layer of organic mulch, around 3-6 inches (7.6-15 cm), around garden beds to insulate the soil and protect plant roots from freezing temperatures. Mulch materials, such as straw, shredded leaves, or bark, help maintain soil moisture and temperature stability.

Wrap Plants

Tender plants and shrubs that are susceptible to cold damage should be wrapped with burlap or frost cloth. This protective layer shields plants from freezing winds and frost, reducing the risk of frostbite on foliage and stems.

Consider Heating and Ventilation

In greenhouses, install heaters or heat mats to maintain a minimum temperature suitable for plants during cold spells. Proper ventilation is important to prevent humidity buildup and fungal diseases while ensuring adequate air circulation.

Provide Water Management

Adjust watering schedules as plants enter dormancy. Reduce watering frequency but ensure plants receive enough moisture to prevent dehydration. Avoid wetting foliage to minimize the risk of frost damage.

Use Cold Frames and Cloches

Utilize cold frames or cloches to create microclimates for protecting sensitive plants. These structures capture and retain solar heat during the day, providing an extra layer of warmth for plants inside.

Monitor Weather and Winter Maintenance

Regularly monitor weather forecasts and greenhouse conditions throughout winter. Remove snow buildup from greenhouse roofs to prevent structural damage and ensure light penetration.

Check plants for signs of stress or pest infestation, addressing issues promptly.

Select Appropriate Plant and Placement

Choose cold-hardy plant varieties suitable for your climate zone. Place more sensitive plants in protected areas or closer to the greenhouse's heat source for added warmth.

Prepare Equipment and Supplies

Stock up on winter gardening supplies, such as frost protection fabrics, heating elements, and tools for snow removal. Having these on hand ensures quick response to weather changes and emergencies.

Adjusting Light and Temperature

Adjusting light and temperature in gardens and greenhouses during winter is crucial to maintain optimal conditions for plant growth and survival.

By implementing these strategies, gardeners can effectively adjust light and temperature in gardens and greenhouses during winter.

Maximize Natural Light

Winter days are shorter with reduced sunlight intensity. Position greenhouse structures to maximize exposure to natural light. Clean greenhouse windows regularly to ensure maximum light transmission. Consider using reflective materials on interior surfaces to bounce light onto your plants.

Provide Supplemental Lighting

Install supplemental lighting systems, such as LED grow lights, to provide adequate light levels during cloudy days and short daylight hours.

LED lights are energy-efficient and emit wavelengths suitable for photosynthesis, promoting healthy plant growth even in low light conditions.

Check Light Duration and Intensity

Monitor daylight hours and adjust artificial lighting schedules accordingly. Most plants require 12-16 hours of light per day for optimal growth. Use timers to automate lighting schedules and maintain consistency in light exposure.

Provide Temperature Regulation

Greenhouses should maintain a stable temperature range conducive to plant health. Use thermometers to monitor internal temperatures and heaters to supplement heat during cold spells. Optimize greenhouse insulation to minimize heat loss and reduce heating costs.

Encourage Ventilation and Air Circulation

Proper ventilation is essential to regulate temperature and humidity levels inside greenhouses. Install vents and fans to facilitate airflow and prevent condensation buildup. Circulating air helps distribute heat evenly and reduces the risk of fungal diseases.

Assess Thermal Mass and Heat Retention

Incorporate thermal mass materials, such as water barrels or stone beds, inside greenhouses. These materials absorb heat during the day and release it at night, stabilizing temperature fluctuations. Covering beds with mulch or row covers also helps retain soil warmth.

Consider Shading and Cooling Systems

During sunny winter days, use shade cloths or adjustable shading systems to prevent overheating inside greenhouses.

Shade cloths reduce light intensity and lower internal temperatures, protecting plants from sunburn and heat stress.

Winterizing Plants to Prevent Shock

Winterizing plants to prevent shock involves several key tips to transition them smoothly into colder seasons, ensuring they survive and thrive despite the challenging conditions.

To effectively winterize your plants and minimize the shock of transitioning into colder seasons, follow these steps.

Allow Gradual Adjustment

Start preparing plants for winter several weeks before the first frost. Gradually reduce watering and fertilizer applications to slow down growth and encourage dormancy. This gradual adjustment helps plants acclimate to changing environmental conditions.

Trim and Prune

Trim back dead or diseased branches and prune overgrown foliage before winter sets in. This not only improves the plant's appearance but also reduces the risk of fungal diseases and improves air circulation, which is crucial during colder, wetter months.

Mulch

Apply a layer of organic mulch 1-2 inch (2.5-5 cm) deep around bushes and 2-3 inch (5-7.6 cm) deep around trees to insulate roots and retain soil moisture.

Mulch acts as a protective barrier against fluctuating temperatures, preventing root damage caused by freezing and thawing cycles. Use materials like shredded leaves, straw, or bark chips for effective insulation.

Provide Protective Coverings

For delicate plants or those marginally hardy in your climate zone, use protective coverings like frost blankets, row covers, or cloches. These structures shield plants from freezing temperatures, windburn, and frost damage while allowing light and air to penetrate.

Monitor Watering

Proper hydration is critical in winter. Water plants deeply before the ground freezes to ensure they enter dormancy with adequate moisture reserves.

During dry winter spells, monitor soil moisture levels and water plants sparingly to prevent dehydration without causing waterlogging.

Move Container Plants

If you have container plants, move them to sheltered areas, such as unheated garages, porches, or indoors near bright windows. Insulate pots with bubble wrap or burlap to protect roots from freezing temperatures. Reduce watering frequency but ensure soil remains slightly moist.

Using Tents and Covers

Using tents and covers effectively requires proactive planning and monitoring to provide optimal protection against frost and cold weather conditions. By employing these techniques, you can safeguard your plants and ensure they remain healthy and productive throughout the challenging winter months. Here's how to utilize covers and tents for safeguarding your plants.

Determine Types of Covers

Choose from various types of covers depending on your plants' needs and the severity of winter conditions. Floating row covers made from lightweight fabrics like polypropylene provide insulation while allowing sunlight, air, and water to permeate.

For more delicate plants or extreme cold, consider using frost blankets or cloches made of plastic or glass, which offer superior insulation and protection.

Ensure Insulation and Heat Retention

Covers and tents create a microclimate around plants, trapping heat radiated from the soil during the day and preventing rapid heat loss at night. This insulation minimizes temperature fluctuations and protects plants from frost damage. Ensure covers are securely anchored to prevent heat loss through gaps and to withstand strong winds.

Consider Ventilation

Proper ventilation is crucial to prevent excessive condensation and fungal diseases. If using plastic covers or cloches, ventilate during sunny days by partially opening or propping them up to allow excess heat and moisture to escape. Monitor humidity levels and adjust ventilation as needed to maintain a healthy environment under covers.

Section 2: Managing Temperature Extremes

Keeping plants cool in summer within greenhouses is important for maintaining optimal growing conditions and preventing heat stress. Here are effective techniques to manage temperature extremes and ensure your plants thrive.

Keeping Plants Cool in Summer

By implementing these techniques, you can effectively manage temperature extremes and create a conducive environment for plant growth within your greenhouse during the hot summer months.

Shade Management

Install shade cloths or screens over greenhouse structures to filter sunlight and reduce solar radiation. Choose shade cloths with varying levels of opacity to customize light transmission based on your plant's specific light requirements. Position shade cloths on the exterior of the greenhouse to block direct sunlight before it reaches the plants.

Ventilation Systems

Implement adequate ventilation systems to promote air circulation and heat dissipation within the greenhouse. Use ridge vents, side vents, or louvers to facilitate natural airflow. Additionally, install exhaust fans or evaporative cooling systems to expel hot air and introduce cooler, fresh air from outside.

Evaporative Cooling

Utilize evaporative cooling techniques, such as misting systems or foggers to lower temperatures inside the greenhouse. These systems release fine droplets of water into the air, which absorb heat as they evaporate, effectively cooling the surrounding environment.

Ensure proper placement and maintenance of misting nozzles to evenly distribute moisture without causing waterlogging.

Thermal Curtains and Screens

Install thermal curtains or screens within the greenhouse to provide insulation and regulate internal temperatures. These curtains can be drawn during the hottest parts of the day to reduce heat transfer and maintain a cooler environment. Opt for reflective or shade screens that deflect sunlight and reduce heat buildup.

Cooling Mats and Flooring

Lay down cooling mats or use porous flooring materials like gravel or concrete to absorb excess heat and maintain stable ground temperatures. Cooling mats made from materials like rubber or woven fabrics can be irrigated with water to enhance cooling efficiency and create a comfortable rooting environment for plants.

Water Management

Implement effective water management practices to prevent soil overheating and maintain plant hydration. Use drip irrigation systems or soaker hoses to deliver water directly to plant roots while minimizing surface evaporation. Mulch soil surfaces with organic materials like straw or bark to retain moisture and regulate soil temperature.

Timed Operations

Schedule greenhouse operations and activities during cooler parts of the day, such as early morning or late evening, to minimize heat stress on plants. Avoid unnecessary openings of the greenhouse during peak sunlight hours to prevent heat influx and maintain internal stability.

Adjusting Ventilation and Airflow

Enhancing airflow and maintaining optimal greenhouse conditions through effective ventilation strategies is important for promoting plant health and productivity.

By implementing these methods to enhance ventilation and airflow in your greenhouse, you can create a healthy and stable growing environment that supports robust plant growth and maximizes crop yields. Here are key methods to adjust ventilation and airflow.

Natural Ventilation

Utilize natural ventilation methods to encourage airflow without relying on mechanical systems. Design your greenhouse with strategically placed vents, windows, and doors that can be opened or closed to regulate airflow based on external weather conditions.

Position vents at both the ridge (roof) and sidewalls to facilitate cross-ventilation, allowing fresh air to enter and hot air to escape.

Mechanical Ventilation Systems

Install mechanical ventilation systems, such as exhaust fans or circulation fans, to enhance airflow and control greenhouse temperatures. Exhaust fans are typically placed at the highest point in the greenhouse to expel hot, stale air, while circulation fans are strategically positioned to promote air movement throughout the growing area.

Consider fans with adjustable speeds to tailor airflow intensity to specific plant requirements.

Louvers and Side Vents

Incorporate adjustable louvers and side vents into your greenhouse design to facilitate controlled airflow. Louvers are slatted panels that can be adjusted to regulate the amount of air entering or leaving the greenhouse.

Side vents provide additional opportunities for air exchange and can be paired with automatic openers or manual controls for precise ventilation management.

Air Circulation Fans

Use air circulation fans strategically placed within the greenhouse to promote uniform airflow and prevent stagnant air pockets. Proper air circulation helps distribute heat, humidity, and carbon dioxide evenly throughout the growing area, ensuring consistent growing conditions for all plants.

Using Shade Cloths and Cooling Systems

By incorporating shade cloths and cooling systems into your greenhouse management practices, you can create a more stable and conducive environment for plant growth. Here's a detailed look at the benefits and application of these systems.

Benefits of Shade Cloths

Using shade cloths and cooling systems in your greenhouse is essential for maintaining optimal growing conditions, especially during periods of intense sunlight and heat. Shade cloths provide several benefits in greenhouse management, including temperature regulation by reducing solar radiation and heat intensity inside the greenhouse.

This helps prevent overheating during hot summer months, which can otherwise stress plants. Additionally, shade cloths diffuse sunlight, providing more uniform light distribution throughout the greenhouse. This reduces hot spots and promotes even growth across all plants.

They also offer protection against harmful ultraviolet (UV) rays, which can damage plant tissues and reduce overall plant health. Furthermore, shade cloths protect delicate plants from sunburn and heat stress, particularly those that are sensitive to high light intensity.

Types of Shade Cloths

Shade cloths are categorized based on their shading percentage, ranging from 30% to 90%. The choice of shade cloth depends on the specific light requirements of your plants and the local climate conditions.

Common materials include woven polyethylene, knitted polypropylene, and aluminum shade cloths. Each material offers varying levels of durability, UV resistance, and heat reflection properties.

Shade cloths are typically installed above the greenhouse roof or directly on the greenhouse structure. They can be fixed permanently or used seasonally depending on weather conditions.

Some shade cloths are designed to be retractable or adjustable, allowing growers to modify shading levels as needed throughout the day or season.

Tailor your shade cloth selection based on crop requirements, considering factors, such as light sensitivity, growth stage, and environmental conditions.

Types of Cooling Systems

Cooling systems complement shade cloths by further enhancing climate control in greenhouses. Some popular cooling systems include evaporative cooling, fan and pad systems, and air conditioning.

Evaporative cooling systems, such as misting or fogging, create a fine mist that evaporates, lowering the greenhouse temperature through latent heat exchange.

Fan and pad systems draw outside air through wet pads, cooling it before distributing it throughout the greenhouse, making them effective in hot and dry climates. In regions with extreme heat, air conditioning units maintain consistent temperatures by removing heat and moisture from the greenhouse air.

Benefits of Temperature Control

Maintaining optimal temperature control in a greenhouse is crucial for ensuring healthy plant growth, maximizing yields, and extending the growing season. Stable temperatures prevent plant stress caused by fluctuations, encouraging steady growth and development.

Each plant species has a preferred temperature range, and climate control helps maintain these optimal conditions, fostering better growth, flowering, and fruiting. High temperatures can cause heat stress, leading to wilting, reduced growth, and even plant death.

Effective cooling systems and shade cloths mitigate these risks, while heaters and thermal screens help maintain a warm environment during colder periods, protecting sensitive plants from cold snaps.

Proper temperature control allows greenhouses to support plant growth throughout the year, regardless of external weather conditions. This is especially beneficial for growing off-season crops, enabling earlier planting in the spring and extending the harvesting period into the fall, thereby increasing productivity and profitability.

Stable temperatures also facilitate efficient photosynthesis, leading to vigorous growth and higher yields. Consistent, optimal temperatures contribute to better fruit set, ripening, and flower development, resulting in superior quality produce and blooms.

Additionally, certain pests also thrive in specific temperature ranges, so controlling the climate can create less favorable conditions for these pests, reducing infestations.

Many plant diseases are exacerbated by temperature extremes and high humidity, so maintaining optimal temperatures helps prevent conditions conducive to disease outbreaks.

Section 3: Maintaining Plant Health During Seasonal Changes

Maintaining plant health through seasonal changes is critical for successful greenhouse gardening. Monitoring plant health and controlling the greenhouse environment effectively are essential strategies to ensure plants thrive year-round.

Monitoring Plant Health

Effective monitoring and control of greenhouse environments are important for maintaining plant health through seasonal changes. By utilizing advanced tools and systems, growers can ensure consistent and optimal conditions, leading to robust plant growth, higher yields, and overall successful greenhouse management.

Manual Monitoring Tools

Thermometers and hygrometers are basic but essential tools for manual monitoring of temperature and humidity. They are useful backups to automated systems and provide quick readings.

Portable CO2 meters are handheld devices measure CO2 levels and are particularly useful in greenhouses without permanent CO2 monitoring systems.

Thermostats and timers are basic climate control tools that can be used to regulate heaters, fans, and lights based on set parameters.

Automated venting systems open and close vents based on temperature and humidity readings, ensuring optimal airflow and preventing heat buildup.

Efficient heating (such as radiant heating) and cooling systems (such as evaporative coolers) are critical for maintaining stable temperatures through seasonal changes.

Soil and Moisture Monitoring

Soil moisture sensors measure the water content in the soil, ensuring that plants receive adequate but not excessive water. Automated irrigation systems can be linked to these sensors for precise watering.

Soil temperature impacts root growth and nutrient uptake. Monitoring soil temperature helps in managing heating systems to maintain optimal root zone temperatures.

Integrated Monitoring Systems

Comprehensive systems integrate various sensors (temperature, humidity, light, CO_2, soil moisture) and provide centralized control. These systems often include remote monitoring capabilities, allowing growers to track conditions via smartphones or computers.

Adjusting Care Routines

Adapting care routines to seasonal changes is crucial for maintaining optimal plant health in a greenhouse. Each season brings different challenges and requirements, necessitating adjustments in watering, feeding, pruning, and overall plant care. Here's a detailed look at how to modify your care routines to ensure your plants thrive throughout the year.

Spring: Awakening and Growth

Spring marks the awakening of plants from their winter dormancy. This season is characterized by increased light and gradually warming temperatures, which spur new growth. As temperatures rise and plants begin to grow, their water needs will increase. It's important to gradually increase watering to match the growing demand.

Maintaining adequate humidity levels to support new growth is also important; using misting systems or placing water trays around the greenhouse can help achieve this.

When it comes to feeding, using a balanced fertilizer to provide essential nutrients as plants start their active growth phase is beneficial. Opting for slow-release fertilizers ensures a consistent nutrient supply.

Prune away any dead or damaged growth from the winter encourages healthy new growth. Support climbing plants or those that need structural training to grow in the desired direction helps manage their development.

Early detection of pests and diseases is vital since warmer weather can lead to higher pest activity. Regular monitoring and using organic pest control methods can help manage any outbreaks effectively.

Summer: Managing Heat and Light

Summer brings intense light and heat, requiring adjustments to prevent plants from overheating and to ensure they receive adequate water. Watering plants more frequently prevents dehydration, with early morning or late evening watering being ideal to reduce evaporation.

Implementing cooling systems, such as shade cloths, fans, and evaporative coolers, helps maintain a manageable temperature within the greenhouse. To support the rapid growth phase, increase the frequency of fertilization is necessary, and using liquid fertilizers allows for quicker nutrient uptake.

Shade management becomes crucial to protect sensitive plants from direct sunlight, preventing sunburn and stress. Regular pruning maintains airflow and prevents overcrowding, which can lead to fungal issues. Checking plants frequently for signs of pests and diseases and removing any affected parts immediately ensures they remain healthy during the intense summer months.

Autumn: Transition and Preparation

Autumn is a transition period where plants begin to slow down their growth as temperatures cool. It's a time to prepare plants for the upcoming winter. As temperatures drop, reducing the frequency of watering prevents waterlogged soil and root rot.

Keeping an eye on humidity levels is essential, as too much moisture can encourage fungal diseases. Gradually reducing the amount of fertilizer as plants' growth slows down is advisable. Switching to a fertilizer with higher potassium content strengthens plants for winter.

Clean up by removing dead leaves and debris to prevent pests and diseases from settling during the winter. Prune plants to remove weak or diseased growth to help them withstand the winter better.

Conducting thorough pest and disease inspections and addressing any issues before winter sets in ensures plants are well-prepared for the colder months.

Winter: Protection and Maintenance

Winter is a critical time for protecting plants from cold temperatures and ensuring they remain healthy despite reduced light and heat. Watering sparingly is important, as plants' water needs are lower in winter.

Ensuring the soil is well-draining avoids waterlogged conditions. Use humidifiers or water trays to help maintain adequate humidity levels without overwatering. Refraining from regular fertilization is important since plants are not actively growing, and excess nutrients can stress them during dormancy.

Supplemental lighting is necessary to compensate for reduced natural light, and using grow lights on timers provides consistent light periods. Maintain a stable temperature using heaters and thermal blankets helps avoid drastic temperature fluctuations.

It is vital to check the greenhouse insulation to retain heat and repairing any gaps or leaks that could let cold air in. Regularly inspecting plants and the greenhouse structure for signs of infestation, even in winter, helps manage any potential pest problems.

Using Seasonal Covers and Protection

Choosing and applying seasonal covers for plant protection is an essential aspect of maintaining a healthy greenhouse environment.

Seasonal covers, such as row covers, frost blankets, and greenhouse films, play a critical role in shielding plants from adverse weather conditions and temperature fluctuations. Proper selection and application of these covers can significantly enhance plant resilience and productivity throughout the year.

Types of Seasonal Covers

Seasonal covers come in various forms, each designed to address specific challenges posed by different seasons. Row covers, typically made from lightweight fabric, are ideal for providing a physical barrier against pests while allowing light and moisture to penetrate.

These covers are particularly useful during the spring and summer months when insect activity is high. Frost blankets, made from thicker, insulating materials, are essential for protecting plants from cold temperatures and frost during autumn and winter.

Greenhouse films, available in various thicknesses and materials, offer year-round protection by regulating temperature and humidity levels inside the greenhouse.

Choosing the Right Cover

Selecting the appropriate seasonal cover depends on the specific needs of your plants and the climatic conditions of your region. For spring and summer, lightweight row covers are effective in protecting young plants from pests and providing a slight temperature boost.

In regions with intense sunlight, shade cloths can be used to reduce heat stress and prevent sunburn. During autumn and winter, thicker frost blankets or thermal covers are necessary to insulate plants from cold temperatures and frost. Greenhouse films with UV protection and anti-drip properties can be used throughout the year to create a stable growing environment.

Applying Seasonal Covers

Proper application of seasonal covers is crucial to ensure their effectiveness. When using row covers, it's important to secure the edges tightly to prevent pests from entering. This can be done using soil, rocks, or fabric staples. Ensure that the covers are not too tight, as this can restrict plant growth and airflow.

For frost blankets, draping them over plants and securing the edges with weights or clips helps trap heat and prevent frost damage. In colder regions, creating a tent-like structure with hoops and securing the frost blankets over the hoops can provide additional insulation.

Greenhouse films should be installed with care to avoid tears and ensure a snug fit. Using greenhouse clips or fasteners helps keep the film in place, especially during windy conditions.

It's important to regularly check and adjust the covers to accommodate plant growth and changing weather conditions.

Removing or adjusting covers during the day allows for adequate light and ventilation, while reapplying them in the evening helps retain heat.

Signs of Stress

Recognizing signs of stress in plants due to weather changes is crucial for maintaining a healthy greenhouse environment. Weather fluctuations, including extreme temperatures, humidity shifts, and sudden changes in light conditions, can impact plant health significantly.

Early identification of stress symptoms allows for timely interventions, helping to prevent long-term damage and ensure optimal plant growth.

Visual Symptoms of Stress

One of the most apparent signs of plant stress is wilting. Wilting can occur when plants do not receive enough water or when they lose more water through transpiration than they can absorb. This is often seen during hot weather or when the humidity levels drop significantly.

Conversely, overwatering can also cause wilting, as it leads to root rot and a lack of oxygen in the soil. Checking the soil moisture levels regularly helps determine the appropriate watering needs of your plants.

Yellowing of leaves, also known as chlorosis, is another common symptom of stress. This can be caused by several factors, including nutrient deficiencies, poor drainage, or overexposure to sunlight.

In cold weather, plants may exhibit discoloration as a response to frost damage or insufficient warmth. Ensuring that your greenhouse environment maintains a balanced nutrient profile and appropriate temperature levels can mitigate these issues.

Leaf scorch or sunburn appears as brown or black spots on the leaves, often caused by intense sunlight or sudden temperature spikes. This condition is more prevalent during the summer when greenhouse temperatures can soar. Using shade cloths or adjusting ventilation can help protect plants from excessive sunlight and heat.

Growth and Developmental Changes

Stressed plants often show stunted growth or abnormal development. For instance, during periods of extreme cold, plants may slow down their growth or halt it altogether. This is a natural response to conserve energy.

However, prolonged exposure to cold temperatures can damage the plant tissues, leading to permanent stunting. Providing supplemental heat during cold spells helps maintain consistent growth rates.

In some cases, plants may produce smaller leaves, flowers, or fruits as a response to stress. This can occur when the plant is under nutritional or environmental stress. Poor root development is another sign, often linked to inadequate soil conditions or improper watering practices.

Ensuring that the soil is well-draining, nutrient-rich, and maintaining consistent watering schedules can support healthy root and plant development.

Chapter Seven
Time for a Harvest – What Now?

WHEN I FIRST STARTED my indoor garden, I was completely mesmerized by the growth process—from tiny seeds sprouting into lush plants bearing fruits. But when it came time to harvest, I found myself at a loss.

How do you know when a tomato is ripe enough to pick? Should cucumbers be left on the vine longer? And once you've gathered your bounty, what's the best way to store it to keep that fresh-from-the-garden taste?

These questions sent me on a quest for knowledge. I scoured gardening guides, tapped into expert advice, and learned from trial and error. Now, I'm eager to share what I've discovered about the art and science of harvesting.

From understanding the subtle signs that indicate peak ripeness to mastering the art of preservation—whether it's freezing berries for winter smoothies or making jams that capture the essence of summer—this chapter dives deep into the practicalities of harvesting and post-harvest care.

Section 1: When and How to Harvest and How to Store

Harvesting your fruits and vegetables is the culmination of all your hard work in the garden. Knowing the right time to harvest ensures you enjoy produce at its peak flavor and nutrition. Each type of fruit or vegetable has its own indicators for ripeness.

Blackberry/Raspberry/Boysenberry

Harvesting

Wait until the berries are fully ripe—this means they should be deep, rich in color, and slightly soft to the touch. For blackberries and boysenberries, you'll need to gently pull the berries off the vine; they should come off easily if they're ripe.

Raspberries, on the other hand, are best picked by gently twisting them from the stem. Use small handheld shears or scissors to avoid damaging the plant. If you're harvesting a lot, a little basket or container will keep your berries safe.

Storage

Fresh berries can be a bit delicate, so handle them with care. Store them in a breathable container lined with paper towels to absorb any excess moisture. If you want to keep them fresh for a bit longer, pop them in the fridge.

For long-term storage, freezing is your best bet. Spread the berries in a single layer on a baking sheet and freeze until solid, then transfer them to a freezer bag. This keeps them from clumping together and makes it easier to grab just what you need!

Blueberry

Harvesting

Blueberries are a breeze to pick! Wait until they turn a deep blue with a frosty grayish bloom. They should feel firm and plump. Gently tug them from the stem—if they come off easily, they're ready. Use small, handheld shears if you're picking a large batch to avoid squishing the delicate berries. A little container or basket will help you transport them without crushing.

Storage

Keep those blueberries fresh by storing them in a breathable container lined with paper towels to soak up any moisture. Refrigerate them to maintain their freshness. For long-term storage, freeze them in a single layer on a baking sheet, then transfer to a freezer bag. This method keeps them from sticking together, so you can easily grab a handful whenever you need.

Cucumber

Harvesting

Cucumbers should be picked when they reach full size and have a nice, glossy green color. They should feel firm and not soft. Use pruning shears or a sharp knife to cut them from the vine, making sure you don't damage the plant. If you have a lot to harvest, a basket or container will keep them from getting squished.

Storage

To keep cucumbers crisp and fresh, store them in the refrigerator. Wrap them in a paper towel or place them in a perforated plastic bag to help maintain humidity. Avoid storing cucumbers with ethylene-producing fruits like apples, as this can make them go soft and bitter.

Grapes

Harvesting

Grapes are best picked when they're at their sweetest! Look for rich color and a slightly sweet taste for red or black grapes. Green grapes should have a slight yellowish hue. Use pruning shears to snip the grape clusters from the vine. Handle them gently to avoid bruising.

Storage

Store grapes in a perforated plastic bag or container in the refrigerator. It's best to wash them just before eating to prevent mold. If you want them to last even longer, you can freeze them for a refreshing,long-lasting snack.

Pepper

Harvesting

Peppers are ready to pick when they've reached their full size and have a rich, glossy color. They should feel firm to the touch. Use pruning shears or scissors to cut the stem, leaving a small piece attached to the fruit to avoid damage. If you're harvesting a bunch, a container or basket will make it easier to carry them without squishing.

Storage

Store peppers in the vegetable crisper drawer of the refrigerator. You can keep them in a produce bag or wrapped in paper to extend their freshness. For long-term storage, consider roasting and freezing them.

Pineapple

Harvesting

Pineapples are a bit of a challenge, but worth it! They're ready to harvest when the fruit turns golden yellow and develops a sweet aroma at the base. It should give slightly when pressed. Use a sharp knife to cut the pineapple from the stem at the base, making sure to get a clean cut to avoid damage.

Storage

If you're eating the pineapple soon, you can store it at room temperature. For longer storage, refrigerate it or cut it into chunks and freeze. Keep the pineapple away from ethylene-producing fruits to prevent it from ripening too quickly.

Strawberry

Harvesting

Strawberries should be picked when they are fully red and have a glossy sheen. They should feel firm and fragrant. Gently twist or cut the stem to avoid damaging the fruit or the plant. Use small shears or scissors for precise cutting if you're harvesting a lot. A container with ventilation will help keep them fresh during transport.

Storage

Store strawberries in the refrigerator immediately to maintain freshness. Keep them in a container with ventilation to prevent moisture buildup. Don't wash them until you're ready to eat, as washing can lead to mold. For longer storage, freeze strawberries after washing, drying, and removing the stems.

Tomato

Harvesting

Tomatoes are ripe and ready to pick when they show a deep color characteristic of their variety and yield slightly to gentle pressure. Harvest them using pruning shears or by gently twisting them off the vine. For large quantities, a container or basket will help transport them without bruising.

Storage

Let tomatoes ripen at room temperature away from direct sunlight. Once ripe, you can store them in the refrigerator to extend their freshness. To maintain flavor, allow tomatoes to come back to room temperature before eating. For long-term storage, canning or making sauces is a great option.

Apple

Harvesting

Dwarf apples are ready to harvest when they are fully colored and firm to the touch. They should detach easily with a gentle twist. Use a sturdy ladder and a picking basket if you're reaching high branches. A gentle twist and pull will help avoid bruising.

Storage

Keep apples in the crisper drawer of the refrigerator to maintain crispness and freshness. They can also be stored at room temperature for a short period. For extended storage, consider canning apples or making applesauce.

Avocado

Harvesting

For indoor avocado trees, pick avocados when they change from green to a darker color and yield slightly to gentle pressure. Use a long pole with a cutting mechanism if the fruit is on a high up branch. Handle them carefully to avoid bruising, as indoor trees may not have large branches.

Storage

Store unripe avocados at room temperature until they're soft. Once ripe, refrigerate them to slow further ripening. To prevent browning after cutting, squeeze a bit of lemon juice on the exposed flesh and store in an airtight container.

Banana

Harvesting

Greenhouse bananas are ready to harvest when they turn yellow with a slight green tip. They should feel firm but not too soft. For home growers,gently twist the bunch from the plant or use a sharp knife to cut them off. Be careful not to damage the plant.

Storage

Keep bananas at room temperature. To slow ripening, you can separate them from the bunch or store them in a cool place. For extended storage, peel and freeze bananas for use in smoothies or baking.

Citrus

Harvesting

Dwarf citrus fruits are ready for harvest when they have a bright,vibrant color and feel firm to the touch. Use hand pruners or clippers to cut the stem close to the fruit, ensuring you don't damage the plant. Gently twist or cut to avoid bruising the fruit.

Storage

Store citrus fruits in a cool, dry place or in the refrigerator to extend their shelf life. A mesh bag can help with airflow. For long-term storage, freeze citrus zest or juice in airtight containers.

Fig

Harvesting

Figs are ripe and ready for harvest when they are soft to the touch and have a deep, rich color. Gently pull or twist the fig from the branch, ensuring you don't damage the plant. A soft touch and care are crucial to avoid bruising the delicate fruit.

Storage

Store fresh figs in the refrigerator in a breathable container lined with paper towels. They are highly perishable, so try to consume them within a few days. For longer storage, consider drying or freezing figs.

Guava

Harvesting

Guavas are ready to harvest when they turn yellow or greenish-yellow and yield slightly to gentle pressure. They should have a fragrant aroma at the stem end. Use pruning shears to cut the stem close to the fruit to avoid damaging the plant.

Storage

Store unripe guavas at room temperature until they ripen. Once ripe, refrigerate them to extend their freshness. For long-term storage, peel and cut guavas into chunks before freezing.

Papaya

Harvesting

Dwarf papayas are ripe and ready to harvest when they turn yellow and give slightly when pressed. Use a sharp knife to cut the fruit from the stem, handling it carefully to avoid bruising. If the fruit is high up, use a ladder or a cutting tool with an extended handle.

Storage

Store unripe papayas at room temperature. Once ripe, refrigerate to maintain freshness. Cut papaya should be stored in an airtight container in the fridge and consumed within a few days.

Soursop

Harvesting

Indoor soursop is ready for harvest when the spikes on the fruit start to soften and turn yellow. The fruit should yield slightly to gentle pressure and have a strong aroma. Use pruning shears or a sharp knife to cut the stem close to the fruit.

Storage

Store soursop at room temperature until ripe, then refrigerate. If not consumed quickly, you can freeze soursop. For cut soursop, use an airtight container to preserve freshness in the refrigerator.

Section 2: Post-Harvest Storage

After the satisfying work of cultivating and harvesting your indoor garden, ensuring that your fruits remain fresh and delicious requires proper storage techniques. This section will guide you through various methods to store your harvested fruits, including short-term storage and long-term preservation through canning.

Short-Term Storage

For those planning to consume their harvest within a short time frame, a few days to a couple of weeks, then short-term storage is often sufficient. Here are the best practices for keeping your fruits fresh:

Refrigeration

Most fruits will stay fresh longer when stored in the refrigerator. However, different fruits have varying temperature and humidity needs. For instance, apples and pears should be stored in a low-humidity drawer, while berries and grapes prefer higher humidity.

Countertops and Cabinets

Some fruits, such as bananas, tomatoes, and citrus fruits, can be stored on the countertop at room temperature. Ensure they are kept away from direct sunlight and other heat sources to prevent premature ripening or spoiling.

Ripening and Ethylene Sensitivity

Be aware that certain fruits emit ethylene gas, which can speed up the ripening of nearby produce. Store ethylene-sensitive fruits like apples and bananas separately to avoid premature ripening.

Long-Term Storage

When you have an abundant harvest or wish to enjoy your garden's fruits year-round, canning is an excellent preservation method. This technique locks in the flavors and nutrients of your fruits, allowing you to savor them long after the growing season ends.

Water Bath Canning

This canning is best used for high-acid fruits such as apples, berries, peaches, and tomatoes.

Fruits are packed into jars, covered with a liquid (such as syrup or juice), and sealed with lids. The jars are then submerged in boiling water for a short period of time to kill any bacteria or microorganisms that could spoil the fruit. Once cooled, the jars form a vacuum seal, preserving the contents for up to a year.

Pressure Canning

These are best with low-acid fruits and fruit mixtures.

This method is similar to water bath canning, but the jars are processed in a pressure canner, which reaches higher temperatures than boiling water. This method is essential for preventing the growth of bacteria and other toxic spores in low-acid foods. The process ensures that your fruits remain safe and preserved for an extended period.

Canning Equipment

Before you start canning, gather the necessary equipment.

Mason jars are the most commonly used for canning. Ensure they are clean, free of cracks, and come with two-piece lids. A flat sealing lid and a screw band.

- Select a canner of choice. Depending on the method, you'll need a water bath canner or a pressure canner.

- A jar lifter or some specialty tool for safely handling hot jars. Never handle heated objects directly by hand.

- Funnels and ladles to help fill the jars without spills.

- A bubble remover or headspace tool to remove air bubbles and measure the correct headspace in the jars.

Canning Process

1. **Prepare the Fruit:** Wash and, if necessary, peel your fruit. Cut into desired sizes or leave whole, depending on the recipe.

2. **Prepare the Jars:** Sterilize jars by placing them in boiling water for 10 minutes. Keep them hot until ready to fill.

3. **Fill the Jars:** Use a funnel to fill the jars with fruit. Add syrup or juice to cover the fruit, again maintaining proper headspace about 1/4 inch (6 mm).

4. **Remove Air Bubbles:** Use a non-metallic tool to remove air bubbles by gently pressing the fruit inside the jar.

5. **Seal the Jars:** Wipe the rims of the jars clean, place the lids on top, and screw on the bands until fingertip tight.

6. **Process the Jars:** Submerge the jars in boiling water, ensuring they are covered by at least 1-2 inches (2.5-5 cm) of water. Boil for the time specified in your recipe.

7. **Cool and Store:** Remove the jars and place them on a towel to cool. After 24 hours, check the seals by pressing the center of each lid. If the lid does not flex, the jar is sealed.

Always label your jars with the date of canning and the contents. This helps you keep track of what needs to be used first.

Store canned fruits in a cool, dark place. Properly canned fruits can last up to a year, but for the best flavor and quality, aim to use them within six months.

Section 3: Preparing for Next Year

I once had so much produce from my indoor garden that I ended up with a mini fruit apocalypse in my kitchen—apples started turning into their own science experiment!

Realizing too late that I needed a game plan, I learned the hard way that preparing for next year isn't just about cleaning up the kitchen, but also about gearing up the garden for its next big debut. So, let's dive into how to avoid the rotting food fiasco and set your garden up for a fantastic comeback!

Clean-Up

As the growing season winds down, the clean-up process is essential for setting the stage fora successful next year. Begin by clearing out any remaining plant debris, which can harbor pests and diseases if left unchecked.

Removing dead plants and fallen leaves not only tidies up your space but also helps prevent potential problems.

For soil that has been used for multiple seasons, consider removing the top layer and replacing it with fresh compost or soil to replenish nutrients.

Disinfecting tools and containers also prevents the spread of disease.

Lastly, if you're using pots or containers, ensure they're cleaned thoroughly before storage to avoid any mold or mildew buildup.

Post-Harvest Care

Once you've harvested your bounty, giving your garden some TLC ensures a smoother transition to the next growing season.

Start by inspecting and cleaning your greenhouse or garden beds, removing any leftover plant material that might attract pests or diseases.

For soil that's been heavily used, consider adding a layer of compost or organic matter to replenish nutrients. If you've used raised beds, rotating your crops is key to preventing soil depletion and controlling pests.

Properly store any garden equipment, cleaning and repairing as needed, to keep them in good shape for the next season. Don't forget to check irrigation systems for any damage or blockages.

Starting the Cycle Again

After a successful harvest, it's always time to prepare for the next cycle of growth,and this stage is all about setting the stage for another fruitful season. Begin by collecting and storing seeds from your best-performing plants, ensuring they're dry and kept in a cool, dark place to maintain their viability.

Next, plan your garden layout for the coming season, considering crop rotation to prevent soil depletion and reduce pest buildup. If you're replanting in the same space, clear out old debris and amend the soil with compost or organic matter to boost its fertility.

Take advantage of the off-season to research new varieties or methods that could enhance your garden's productivity. Preparing your garden now, with a clear plan and healthy soil, ensures that you're ready to hit the ground running when planting season arrives.

This proactive approach not only helps in preventing future problems but also sets you up fora vibrant and productive growing season.

Soil Preparation

Soil preparation is like giving your garden a hearty breakfast before it starts its day. After the harvest, the first step is to clear away any leftover plant debris and weeds that might harbor pests or diseases.

Next, it's crucial to test your soil to check its pH and nutrient levels. This will help you understand what amendments your soil might need. For most indoor or greenhouse gardens, enriching the soil with compost or well-rotted manure will add essential nutrients and improve soil structure.

If you're dealing with compacted soil, consider incorporating organic matter to enhance drainage and aeration. Additionally, turning the soil helps to integrate these amendments evenly. If you're preparing for a new growing season, it might be beneficial to use cover crops during the off-season.

These plants not only help prevent soil erosion but also add nutrients back into the soil when tilled under. By investing time in soil preparation, you're ensuring that your garden will be fertile and ready to support vigorous plant growth when you start planting again.

Crop Rotation

Crop rotation is like giving your garden a strategic game plan to keep it in top shape year after year. By rotating crops, you avoid planting the same type of vegetable or fruit in the same soil consecutively. This helps prevent soil depletion, reduces the risk of pests and diseases, and improves soil fertility.

For indoor or greenhouse gardens, where space is often limited, rotate crops between containers or different sections of your garden. For instance, if you grew tomatoes in one container, plant leafy greens or root vegetables in that space the following season.

This practice helps break the life cycles of pests and diseases that thrive on specific plants. Additionally, using a crop rotation plan ensures that you are maximizing the benefits of each plant type, as legumes, for example, can fix nitrogen in the soil, benefiting subsequent crops.

Keep in mind that successful rotation involves planning and keeping records of what you planted where, so you can ensure a balanced and healthy garden ecosystem.

Checking Plant Health

Keeping tabs on plant health is like regular check-ups for your garden. Routine inspections ensure your plants stay robust and resilient throughout their growth. Start by visually examining plants for signs of stress, such as yellowing leaves,wilting, or unusual spots, which might indicate issues like nutrient deficiencies or diseases.

Check the soil moisture to avoid over- or under-watering, as both can stress plants. Regularly inspect for pests like aphids or spider mites that can damage plants and spread diseases. Using tools like moisture meters, pH testers, and plant health checkers can help you monitor soil conditions and plant health more accurately.

For a more thorough approach, consider using automated systems that provide real-time data on temperature, humidity, and other vital factors. These tools help you adjust conditions promptly, maintaining optimal plant health. By keeping a close eye on your plants and their environment, you ensure a thriving garden ready for a successful next season.

Chapter Eight
What Comes Next

AFTER SUCCESSFULLY STORING MY first bountiful harvest, I found myself drowning in an ocean of blueberries, tomatoes, and cucumbers. There's only so much you can eat, right?

So, with a fridge bursting at the seams and friends politely declining any more "generous" produce gifts, I had a wild idea: why not sell some of this?

What started as a casual weekend venture quickly spiraled into a full-blown hobby-turned-business. My little greenhouse became a bustling enterprise, and I was suddenly juggling customer demands, pricing strategies, and thinking about year-round production.

In this chapter, I'll share how to take your passion for indoor gardening to the next level. From setting up a legit business and identifying which fruits are hot sellers, to mastering continuous production techniques and cutting costs without sacrificing quality, I've got you covered.

Just remember, while turning your garden into a profitable venture sounds dreamy, it requires a bit of planning, a dash of business savvy, and a whole lot of love for those little green wonders. Let's dive in!

Section 1: Monetizing Your Indoor Garden

Ever thought about making your indoor garden pay for itself? I did, and next thing I knew, I was the proud owner of a small produce empire (okay, maybe more like a corner stand at the local farmer's market).

In this section, we'll explore how to turn your green thumb into green cash. From setting up your garden business and finding out which fruits are hot sellers, to mastering the art of selling and pricing like a pro, you'll get all the juicy details to start making money from your hobby. Who knew that homegrown tomatoes could pay the bills?

Setting Up a Business

Turning your garden into a business might sound daunting, but it's easier than you think.

First, make sure to check local regulations because selling produce without the proper paperwork could lead to some awkward conversations with your neighbors and the health department.

Once you're legal, set up a dedicated space for your garden business, whether it's a small greenhouse or a corner of your backyard.

Next, create a business plan. I know, I know—"business plan" sounds boring, but it's essential. Outline what you'll grow, your target market, and your budget.

Consider starting small with a few high-demand fruits like tomatoes, strawberries, or peppers. Trust me, there's a big market for fresh, organic produce.

Don't forget to brand your business. A catchy name and a fun logo can go a long way. And finally, get online.

Use social media to showcase your beautiful produce and connect with potential customers. Before you know it, you'll be the talk of the town, and those produce will practically sell themselves!

Identifying Fruits in Demand

Choosing the right fruits to grow is like picking the best contestants for a reality show—some will win over everyone's hearts, and some will flop. To avoid any drama, start by researching which fruits are hot commodities in your local market.

Tomatoes, strawberries, and peppers are almost always in high demand because they're staples in many households. But don't overlook more niche options like blueberries and grapes, which can also bring in a steady stream of customers looking for something special.

Check out local farmers' markets to see what's selling quickly and chat with other growers about their experiences. Online resources and gardening forums are also  gold mines for figuring out what's trending in the fruit world.

Remember, growing what people want to buy means fewer leftovers for your compost pile and more cash in your pocket. Plus, the more popular your produce, the more likely you'll be able to charge premium prices. Just imagine, your blueberries becoming the Beyoncé of the farmers' market—irresistible and always in demand!

Selling Strategies and Marketing

So, you've got a bounty of luscious fruits—now what? Time to don your marketing hat and get those fruits flying off the shelves. Start by creating a brand that stands out. A catchy name and a simple logo can make a huge difference.

Think about setting up a social media presence where you can share mouth-watering photos of your produce and updates about your garden. Engage with your followers by posting recipes, gardening tips, or behind-the-scenes looks at your growing process.

Farmers' markets are your best friend. They're perfect for meeting customers face-to-face and building a loyal clientele. Don't forget to offer samples; once people taste your juicy strawberries or crisp apples, they'll be hooked.

Another strategy is to partner with local restaurants or grocery stores. Many places love to boast about using locally sourced ingredients, and your high-quality produce can become a key selling point for them.

Lastly, consider setting up a subscription box service. Customers love the convenience of having fresh, seasonal fruits delivered to their doorstep. Plus, it gives you a predictable income stream. Marketing your produce isn't just about selling; it's about creating a community of fruit fans who'll keep coming back for more.

Pricing Your Produce

 Ah, pricing—it's like the Goldilocks dilemma of the gardening world. Too high, and you'll scare off customers; too low, and you'll barely cover costs. Finding that just-right price requires a bit of finesse.

Start by researching your local market to see what other growers are charging for similar produce. Farmers' market stalls, local grocery stores, and even online marketplaces can give you a ballpark figure.

Consider your costs, including seeds, water, soil, and time. Don't forget to factor in any unique selling points, like organic certification or rare fruit varieties. Premium products can command higher prices, especially if you emphasize their quality and freshness.

Offering different pricing tiers can also be a smart move. Bulk discounts or subscription services can entice regular buyers and create steady income.

A key strategy is to keep an eye on the seasons. Prices for fruits can fluctuate based on availability, so adjust your rates accordingly. Don't be afraid to start on the higher side and adjust based on customer feedback.

Clear, transparent pricing helps build trust with your customers, ensuring they feel they're getting good value for their money. So, whip out that calculator and find your sweet spot!

Section 2: Continuous Production Techniques

So, you've got the hang of selling your produce, but how do you keep the goods coming year-round? Welcome to the world of continuous production, where your garden keeps giving, no matter the season.

We'll dive into prepping for year-round production and creating a killer growing schedule that maximizes your profits and keeps those customers coming back for more. Because let's face it, nothing screams "business savvy" like a constant supply of fresh avocados in the middle of winter.

Preparing for Year-Round Production

If you thought your greenhouse was just a seasonal hobby, think again! With a bit of planning and a few tweaks, you can turn it into a year-round operation. The key is to adapt to the changing seasons and keep your plants happy no matter what the weather throws at you.

First, consider investing in some good insulation and heating options. A well-insulated greenhouse retains heat better, making it more energy-efficient and cost-effective.

Next, think about the crops you want to grow throughout the year. Certain fruits, like tomatoes and peppers, thrive in the warmer months, while others, like leafy greens and certain herbs, do well in cooler temperatures. Creating a planting calendar can help you schedule when to plant each crop so you always have something growing.

Also, don't underestimate the power of artificial lighting. As daylight hours shorten, supplemental lighting can keep your plants photosynthesizing and growing strong. Proper ventilation and humidity control are also crucial, especially during the winter months when condensation can become an issue.

Lastly, keep an eye on your greenhouse's microclimate. Monitoring tools like thermometers and hygrometers can help you maintain the perfect environment for your plants year-round. With these steps, you can enjoy fresh produce from your greenhouse no matter the season!

Scheduling for Maximum Yield

Ever wished you could hit the "fast-forward" button on your plants to get a harvest faster? While that magical button doesn't exist, a well-planned schedule can feel pretty close. The trick is to map out a planting calendar that maximizes your greenhouse's potential throughout the year.

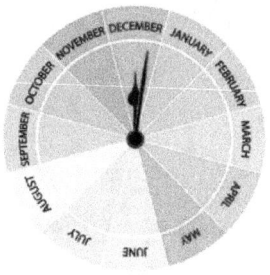

Start by considering the growth cycles of the fruits and vegetables you're growing. For instance, fast-growing crops like radishes and greens can be rotated more frequently, giving you multiple harvests per year.

On the other hand, slower-growing plants like tomatoes and peppers need a bit more patience, so plan their planting dates accordingly to ensure they hit their peak during the right season.

Be sure to account for the greenhouse's climate conditions. Some crops may thrive better in cooler weather, while others need consistent warmth. Planning your planting and harvesting around these needs will help you avoid bottlenecks and ensure your plants are always in their prime.

Don't forget to factor in time for any maintenance or adjustments. Regularly check your greenhouse's environment and make any necessary tweaks to keep things running smoothly. With a solid schedule and a little bit of foresight, your greenhouse will be the gift that keeps on giving all year long.

Section 3: Lower Costs and Higher Efficiency

Running a profitable garden business isn't just about growing the best produce; it's also about being smart with your resources. This section is all about cutting costs and boosting efficiency.

We'll look at some clever homemade solutions, the latest tech investments to get better yields, and how to balance your spending to ensure those investments actually pay off. Get ready to become the thrifty gardener who knows how to squeeze every last cent out of those cucumbers!

Reducing Costs with Homemade Solutions

Ever find yourself staring at your utility bill and wondering if your greenhouse is secretly running a small country? It's time to get creative with homemade solutions to trim those expenses without sacrificing plant happiness.

Start with DIY energy-saving hacks, like crafting your own insulating greenhouse covers from old blankets or bubble wrap. Not only do these materials trap heat efficiently, but they also give you a fun, eco-friendly project. If you're handy, consider building your own rainwater collection system to keep those pesky water bills in check.

Another trick is to repurpose old materials for your greenhouse. Those plastic containers you've been hoarding? Turn them into plant pots. Old pallets can become sturdy shelving. Not only does this keep costs low, but it also gives you a bit of that crafty, resourceful gardener vibe.

Implementing these homemade solutions doesn't just save you money; it also adds a personal touch to your greenhouse. So, put on your DIY hat, get inventive, and watch those savings grow along with your plants.

Investing in Technology for Better Yield

Ever wish your greenhouse could double as a sci-fi movie set? Well, with the right technology, it practically can! Investing in modern greenhouse tech might sound like a futuristic fantasy, but it's more about practical upgrades that turn your plant-growing space into a high-efficiency oasis.

Start with climate control systems like automated vents and temperature regulators. These gadgets ensure your plants stay comfortable without requiring you to constantly monitor them.

Next, consider investing in LED grow lights. They're energy-efficient and provide the perfect spectrum for plant growth, making those nighttime hours just as productive as the day.

Don't overlook smart irrigation systems either. They deliver just the right amount of water, reducing waste and saving you from the daily watering chore.

If you're feeling particularly high-tech, look into greenhouse management software. It helps track plant health, growth patterns, and even financials, so you can focus on the fun stuff—like talking to your plants.

Upgrading to these technologies not only boosts your yield but also makes you look like the coolest, most tech-savvy gardener on the block. So go ahead, embrace the future, and watch your plants—and profits—flourish!

Balancing Investment with Returns

Diving into greenhouse upgrades is like embarking on a high-stakes game of Monopoly—except the properties are plants, and the "bank" is your wallet. Balancing investment with returns requires a bit of savvy strategizing. You don't want to end up with a shiny new greenhouse setup but a balance sheet that's as empty as your compost bin after a week of overzealous gardening.

Start by carefully evaluating the cost of each upgrade. Fancy new climate controls or automated watering systems might sound like a dream, but ensure they'll truly boost your yield and offset their costs.

Next, calculate the potential increase in revenue from these upgrades. For instance, improved lighting and climate control can enhance plant growth and quality, leading to higher sales prices.

It's also crucial to monitor the impact of your investments over time. Are your new upgrades paying off? If your upgraded systems are producing bountiful crops and helping you fetch better prices, then you're on the right track. But if the returns aren't stacking up as expected, it might be time to reassess your strategy.

Remember, while investing in your greenhouse can be thrilling, staying grounded in financial reality ensures your garden grows not just in size, but in profitability too.

Please Leave a Quick Review

Customer reviews

★★★★★ 5 out of 5 ⌄

14 customer ratings

5 star		100%
4 star		0%
3 star		0%
2 star		0%
1 star		0%

Review this product

Share your thoughts with other customers

Write a customer review

THANK YOU SO MUCH for your time. If you enjoyed this book and felt that it helped you gain more confidence as a gardener, I would greatly appreciate if you can take just 60 seconds to please leave a review on Amazon. As an independent author, reviews are my livelihood on this platform. It can be a few sentences. Please enjoy your amazing gardening journey beginning from dirt to harvest!

Conclusion

IMAGINE THIS...IT'S A YEAR later from finishing this book. As you sip your morning coffee, basking in the soft glow of your indoor garden's lighting, you might find yourself reflecting on how far you've come.

Remember that first seed you planted? It felt like such a tiny, insignificant start, nestled in a pot with high hopes and dreams of leafy greens and vibrant fruits.

And fast forward to today, you're now surrounded by a thriving jungle of produce, each plant a testament to your patience and skill. Who knew that a few humble seeds could grow into such a lush and bountiful oasis?

The journey from sprouting seeds to harvesting ripe fruit is more than just a botanical process – it's a transformative experience. You've navigated the intricacies of indoor gardening, mastered the art of controlling climate, and turned your space into a verdant sanctuary. Starting up all of it within 30 days!

Every step, from setting up your greenhouse to ensuring optimal conditions, has been a piece of a larger puzzle, building towards this incredible moment of harvest.

Now, let's talk about that harvest. There's nothing quite like the feeling of plucking a ripe tomato off the vine or gathering a handful of sweet strawberries. But as gratifying as it is to harvest, it's just the beginning.

The true test of your gardening prowess comes after the fruits of your labor are gathered. Proper storage becomes paramount – because let's face it, no one wants a fridge full of rotting produce. With the right techniques, you can extend the freshness of your harvest, from crisp cucumbers to succulent peppers, and savor your garden's bounty for weeks to come.

Imagine enjoying a fresh fruit salad made with your own hand-picked produce, all thanks to a bit of planning and preservation.

And here's where things get really exciting: the potential to turn your gardening passion into a full-fledged business. As you gaze at your flourishing garden, it might dawn on you that your green thumb could be more than just a hobby. What if you could share your home-grown treasures with others?

Setting up a small business around your produce is not just a possibility – it's a real opportunity. Start by considering how you might market your fruits and vegetables. Local farmers' markets, online platforms, or even subscription boxes could be your ticket to turning your gardening hobby into a profitable venture.

Identifying which fruits and vegetables are in high demand will give you an edge. You'll need to stay tuned to market trends, finding out what people crave and adjusting your offerings accordingly.

When it comes to selling, strategy is key. Crafting effective marketing tactics can make or break your business. Think of creative ways to showcase your produce – vibrant photos, engaging social media posts, and eye-catching labels can all attract attention.

Pricing is another crucial element. Setting the right price for your produce involves balancing cost and perceived value. You want to ensure your prices cover your expenses while still being attractive to buyers. Researching pricing strategies and understanding market rates will help you make informed decisions.

But wait, there's more! What if you want to keep your garden producing all year long? Transitioning to year-round production might seem daunting, but with the right preparation, it's entirely feasible.

Planning your growing calendar to include crops that thrive in different seasons can keep your greenhouse bustling with activity. From winter greens to hardy root vegetables, there are plenty of options to keep your garden productive throughout the year. Proper scheduling will ensure you're not only making the most of your space but also maximizing your yield. I created a bonus planner that will assist you on your gardening journey. You can download it free on my website at www.gregorysgardens.com

And let's not overlook cost management. Running a greenhouse involves expenses, but there are plenty of ways to reduce costs without sacrificing quality. DIY solutions can be surprisingly effective—from homemade compost bins to energy-efficient heating methods, there's a lot you can do to keep expenses in check. Investing in technology can also boost efficiency and yield.

Smart sensors, automated watering systems, and advanced climate control can all contribute to a more productive and cost-effective operation.

However, balancing investment with returns is crucial. It's tempting to splurge on the latest gadgets or make ambitious upgrades, but it's important to weigh these investments against their potential benefits.

Prioritize upgrades that offer clear advantages and align with your long-term goals. Thoughtful investment will pay off in the form of improved productivity and increased profits.

As you look ahead, remember that your indoor garden isn't just a space for growing plants – it's a gateway to endless possibilities. With some thoughtful planning and a bit of entrepreneurial spirit, you can turn your gardening passion into something truly extraordinary.

Whether you're perfecting your harvest techniques, exploring business opportunities, or seeking ways to maximize efficiency, every step you take brings you closer to realizing your green dreams.

So, as you plot your next steps, keep this in mind: the path from a simple hobby to a thriving business is paved with creativity, hard work, and a touch of ingenuity. Embrace the challenges and savor the victories, knowing that with the right approach, your garden can evolve into a flourishing enterprise.

Dive into the world of possibilities with confidence, and watch as your green dreams take root and blossom.

The adventure of indoor gardening has just begun—and the best is yet to come. As you step into the future of your green endeavors, whether you envision a serene personal oasis or a thriving business, remember this: the world is your greenhouse, and endless possibilities are sprouting just beneath the surface.

With every plant you nurture, every seed you sow, you're not just cultivating produce; you're crafting a unique story of growth, resilience, and innovation.

The journey from a simple hobby to a flourishing enterprise is like tending to a garden – it takes patience, dedication, and a sprinkle of creativity. So, roll up your sleeves, embrace the dirt, and let your enthusiasm blossom.

Dive into the planning, the strategizing, and the planting with zest. Each challenge you face is an opportunity to grow stronger, and each success, a testament to your hard work.

Whether you're perfecting your harvest methods, exploring new ways to market your produce, or scaling up your operations, remember that every step forward is a step toward realizing your green dreams.

The journey is yours to shape, full of twists and turns, triumphs and lessons. Embrace the adventure with open arms, knowing that with every effort you make, you're cultivating not just a garden, but a future brimming with potential.

So here's to you—the gardener, the innovator, the dreamer. Let your passion guide you, your creativity inspire you, and your commitment drive you forward. The fruits of your labor are not only ready to shine; they're ready to illuminate the path to your future.

Go ahead, plant those seeds, nurture those dreams, and watch as your vision blooms into reality. The garden of tomorrow awaits, and it's going to be spectacular.

If you enjoyed this book and felt that it helped you gain more confidence as a gardener, I would appreciate it if you can take a few minutes to please a leave a review on Amazon. Enjoy your amazing gardening journey beginning from dirt to harvest!

Other Gardening Works

Here are my other books that will help you on your path to being a more independent gardener. Available now on Amazon.

Buy on Amazon Now

Buy on Amazon Now

Your Free Gift

Your gardening bonus on how you can budget, design, and organize your garden in less than 30 days is available now! Using the guide along with this book will help you to start your garden off strong. Download it for free at the website below:

www.gregorysgardens.com

Glossary

GARDENING TERMS CAN SOMETIMES be a little daunting. If some terms are already familiar to you, congratulations! You are definitely growing as a gardener.

Aeroponics

A soil-less cultivation method where plants grow with their roots suspended in air, receiving a nutrient mist. This technique, ideal for indoor gardens, promotes rapid growth and efficient nutrient absorption.

Business Plan

A detailed document outlining the strategy for starting and operating a gardening-related business. It includes market analysis, financial projections, and operational plans, crucial for turning a hobby into a profitable venture.

Composting

The process of decomposing organic matter, such as kitchen scraps and yard waste, into nutrient-rich soil. Improves soil health and reduces waste, essential for maintaining a thriving indoor garden.

Chlorosis

A yellowing of normally green leaves due to a lack of chlorophyll. The may result from various factors that include nutrient deficiencies, drought, poor drainage, and compaction of the soil.

Crop Demand

The level of consumer interest in specific types of produce. Identifying high-demand crops helps in planning what to grow for maximum profitability and market appeal.

Crop Rotation

A strategy where different plant species are grown in the same area in successive seasons to prevent soil depletion and reduce pest and disease build-up. In greenhouses, this technique helps maintain soil fertility and optimize plant health.

Energy Efficiency

Efforts to reduce energy consumption in greenhouse operations. This includes using energy-efficient equipment, optimizing heating and cooling systems, and implementing conservation practices.

Greenhouse

A controlled-environment structure used for growing plants. It regulates temperature, humidity, and light to create optimal conditions year-round, allowing for consistent growth and extended growing seasons.

Greenhouse Climate Control

Management of temperature, humidity, and light within a greenhouse to create ideal growing conditions. Effective climate control systems help optimize plant growth and ensure consistent production.

Greenhouse Management

The activities involved in operating and maintaining a greenhouse. Effective management includes monitoring environmental conditions, managing plant care, and ensuring efficient use of resources.

Greenhouse Upgrade

Enhancements made to a greenhouse to improve its efficiency or functionality. Upgrades might include installing better climate control systems, improving insulation, or adding advanced lighting.

Harvest Scheduling

Planning the timing and order of harvesting different crops to maximize freshness and yield. Effective harvest scheduling helps in managing labor and optimizing produce quality.

Harvesting

The act of collecting mature fruits, vegetables, or herbs from plants. Proper techniques ensure produce is gathered at peak ripeness and handled correctly to maintain quality.

Hydroponics

A method of growing plants in a nutrient-rich water solution without soil. Common in indoor gardens, which allows for precise control of nutrient levels and water usage, often resulting in faster plant growth.

Indoor Garden

A gardening setup inside a building, which could be a dedicated space or integrated into living areas. Indoor gardens can utilize various systems like hydroponics or soil-based methods to grow herbs, vegetables, and fruits.

Indoor Growing Systems

Different setups used for growing plants indoors, including hydroponics, aeroponics, and vertical gardens. These systems allow for year-round cultivation and efficient space utilization.

Integrated Pest Management (IPM)

A holistic approach to pest control that combines biological, cultural, physical, and chemical methods. IPM aims to manage pests effectively while minimizing environmental impact and chemical use.

Market Research

The process of analyzing consumer preferences, market trends, and competition to make informed decisions about product offerings and business strategies. Doing so helps in positioning products effectively and identifying opportunities.

Nutrient Solution

A water mixture with essential nutrients delivered to plants in hydroponic and aeroponic systems. It provides all necessary elements for plant growth and development, tailored to the needs of different crops.

Organic Certification

The process of verifying that produce meets organic standards and regulations. Certification ensures that products are grown according to organic farming principles, including the prohibition of synthetic chemicals.

Organic Produce

Fruits and vegetables grown without synthetic pesticides, herbicides, or genetically modified organisms (GMOs). Organic gardening practices focus on using natural fertilizers and pest control methods.

Pest Control

Methods used to manage and reduce pests that can harm plants. Some techniques include biological controls, physical barriers, and targeted chemical treatments to protect plant health.

Plant Health Monitoring

Regular observation of plants to detect issues, such as diseases, pests, and nutrient deficiencies. Monitoring plant health helps in early intervention and maintaining optimal growth.

Plant Nutrition

The study of how plants absorb and utilize nutrients from soil or growing mediums. Proper plant nutrition is vital for healthy growth, productivity, and overall plant health.

Plant Varieties

Different types of plants with distinct characteristics, such as flavor, growth habits, and disease resistance. Selecting the right varieties is crucial for achieving desired results in indoor gardens and greenhouses.

Post-Harvest Care

The procedures followed after harvesting produce to maintain its quality and extend shelf life. This includes cleaning, sorting, packaging, and storing produce properly to prevent spoilage.

Pricing Strategy

The approach used to determine the selling price of produce. Pricing should consider production costs, market demand, and competitor prices to ensure profitability.

Pruning

The selective removal of specific parts of a plant, such as branches or leaves, to enhance growth, improve air circulation, and increase fruit or flower production. Regular pruning is crucial for maintaining plant health and productivity.

Ripeness

The optimal stage of maturity for fruits and vegetables when they are at their peak flavor, texture, and nutritional value. Indicators of a ripe fruit varies by fruit type and include color, firmness, and aroma.

Seed Germination

The process by which seeds sprout and develop into seedlings. Successful germination requires specific conditions, such as temperature, moisture, and light. It is the first step in growing healthy plants.

Soil Fertility

The ability of soil to provide essential nutrients for plant growth. Improving such involves adding organic matter, adjusting pH levels, and ensuring balanced nutrient availability.

Soil Preparation

The process of preparing the soil or growing medium for planting by enhancing its texture, fertility, and drainage. This may involve mixing in compost, adjusting pH levels, and ensuring proper aeration.

Sustainable Gardening

Practices focused on environmental stewardship and resource conservation. Such methods include composting, water conservation, and using organic pest control to support long-term plant health and reduce ecological impact.

Transpiration

The process of water movement through a plant and its evaporation to leaves, stems, and flowers. It is a passive process that requires no energy that also cools plants.

Ventilation

The system of exchanging indoor air with fresh outdoor air in a greenhouse. Proper ventilation helps control temperature, humidity, and air quality, creating an optimal environment for plant growth.

Vertical Gardening

A technique of growing plants upwards using structures like trellises or wall-mounted planters. This approach maximizes space in indoor gardens and is especially useful in urban settings where ground space is limited.

Watering Techniques

Various methods used to deliver water to plants, including drip irrigation, hand watering, and automated systems. Effective watering techniques are essential for ensuring plants receive the right amount of moisture.

Yield

The quantity of produce harvested from a garden or greenhouse. It can be influenced by plant variety, growing conditions, and cultivation practices, and is a key metric for assessing productivity.

Yield Optimization

Strategies and techniques to maximize the amount of produce harvested. This may involve adjusting growing conditions, selecting high-yield varieties, and improving nutrient management.

Zoning

The division of a garden or greenhouse into different areas based on specific growing conditions or plant requirements. Zoning helps optimize space and resource use, allowing for better plant management.

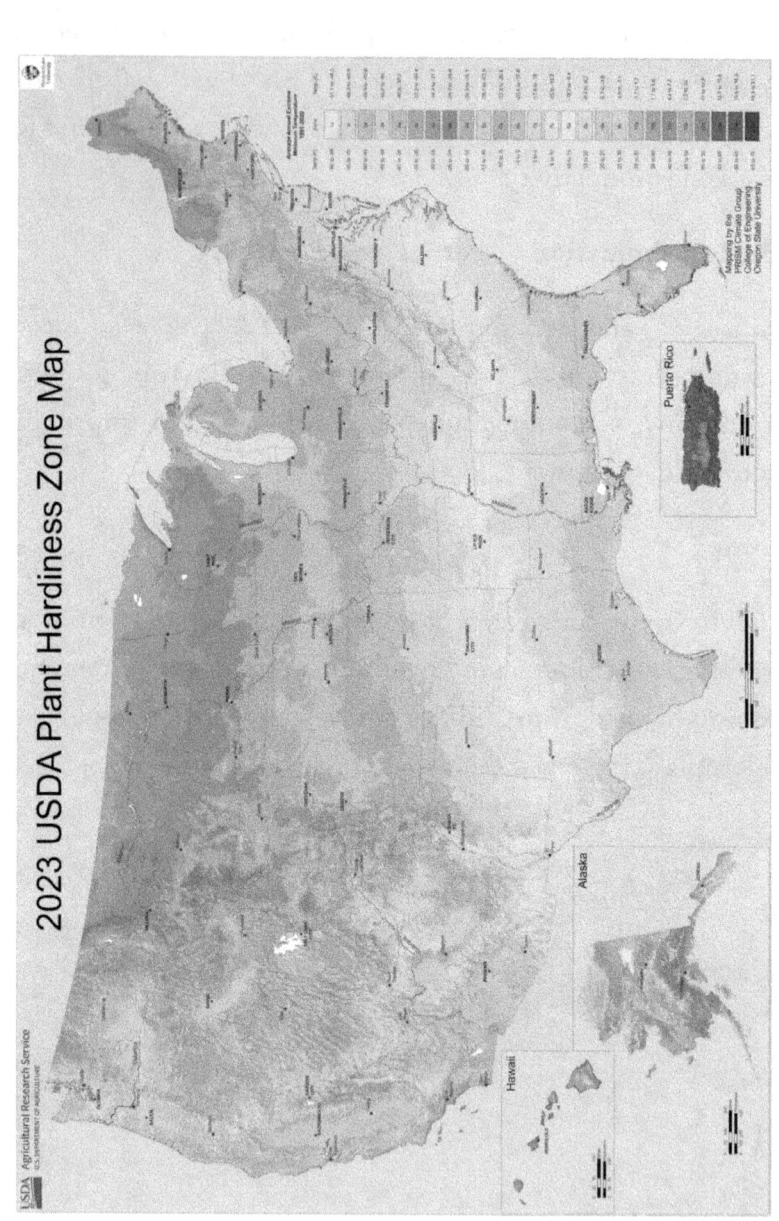

2023 USDA Plant Hardiness Zone Map